For Charles Kelly,
  Who may find <u>Dinarbas</u> (though not <u>Rasselas</u>) worth collecting.
    Cordially,
         Gevin

May 15, 1998

DINARBAS

Ellis Cornelia Knight

DINARBAS

Edited by Ann Messenger

EAST LANSING
COLLEAGUES PRESS
1993

Early Women Writers 1650–1800: No. 2

ISBN 0-937191-49-3
Library of Congress Catalog Number 92-74222
British Library Cataloguing-in-Publication data available
Copyright 1992 by Ann Messenger
All rights reserved

Published by Colleagues Press Inc.
Post Office 4007
East Lansing, Michigan 48826

Distributed outside North America by
Boydell and Brewer Ltd.
Post Office Box 9
Woodbridge, Suffolk IP12 3DF
United Kingdom

Printed in the United States of America

CONTENTS

Foreword vii

Editor's Introduction 1

DINARBAS;
  a Tale; Being a Continuation of Rasselas, Prince of Abissinia

Introduction 9

Contents 11

Text 13

FOREWORD

Avowedly a "continuation" of Samuel Johnson's *Rasselas*, Ellis Cornelia Knight's *Dinarbas* initially attained public physical closeness to its famous predecessor in 1792, when a Philadelphia printer bound together his 1791 (the second American) edition of *Rasselas* and his 1792 (the first American) edition of *Dinarbas*. Subsequently, aside from their discrete publication, the two works appeared together intermittently until 1845, the date of an edition issued in Manchester and Liverpool. Thereafter, the tales went their separate ways. *Rasselas*, of course, has been in print continuously from its publication in 1759 up to the present time. *Dinarbas*, on the other hand, apparently came out last a full century ago (London: C. Dilly, 1892).

Thus, a new edition of Cornelia Knight's sequel to Johnson's "history" (at the end of which, we are told, "nothing is concluded") constitutes a notable, very welcome addition, both for professional and common readers, to easily accessible eighteenth-century texts. Specialists can readily discern the enhanced opportunities for a variety of scholarly studies which this edition provides. Doubtless like most other teachers of eighteenth-century fiction, I am particularly gratified that undergraduates and graduate students, instead of merely hearing a brief description of its contents, can now be asked to read and compare *Dinarbas* with *Rasselas* and (say) Voltaire's *Candide*.

The three stories – a novel-apologue, an apologue (as Ann Messenger classifies the first two) and a *conte philosophique* (as *Candide* is usually labeled) – address matters of fundamental concern to all members of our extraordinary species: the nature of human beings and their constant efforts to secure happiness in a world supposedly created by a benevolent, omniscient, and omnipotent deity but filled with physical and moral evil. *Candide* and *Rasselas*, readers have generally agreed, offer decidedly pessimistic assessments of the human predicament. But in the Introduction to her "continuation," Miss Knight, concurring with the widespread response to *Rasselas*, states that she has consciously presented a "fairer prospect" of humanity than that delineated by Johnson.

FOREWORD

The remarkable popularity of *Candide* and *Rasselas*, accompanied by the lengthy neglect of *Dinarbas*, might seem to suggest that audiences are more attracted to somber estimates of the human comedy than to bright prospects. However, over the years I have found, among undergraduates at least, the number of "optimist" readers of *Rasselas* (i.e., those who call its lesson excessively gloomy) considerably larger than the number of "pessimist" readers (i.e., those who praise the accuracy of its lesson). Yet the "optimists" have often lamented the absence of a fictional narrative of the same historical period they could examine and cite as an explicit counterbalance to the dark vision of *Rasselas* and *Candide*, which, they say, exceeds *Rasselas* in its exaggeration of the human plight.

This fresh edition of *Dinarbas* eminently fulfills their wishes. So, on their behalf and in expectation of many ensuing classroom discussions, spirited and fruitful, of our race's unremitting pursuit of happiness in an imperfect world, I express warm thanks to everyone associated with, and responsible for, the admirable publication.

Gwin J. Kolb

EDITOR'S INTRODUCTION

SAMUEL JOHNSON'S *Rasselas* ends with "The Conclusion, in Which Nothing is Concluded," as his travellers, still daydreaming of happiness but knowing their dreams cannot be obtained, prepare to return to Abyssinia. The openness of the ending has provoked much critical debate over Johnson's motives and meanings. His friend and biographer, Sir John Hawkins, had no doubt as to the ending's purpose, however: Johnson was planning a sequel "in which he meant to marry his hero, and place him in a state of permanent felicity." But he never did, because he discovered "that in this state of our existence all our enjoyments are fugacious, and permanent felicity unattainable" (Hawkins, 157).

Hawkins was not alone in reading *Rasselas* as a wholly dark picture of human experience, although modern critics debate the point vigorously. Another acquaintance of Johnson's had the same reaction, and, disagreeing with such a view of life, took steps to redress the balance.

Ellis Cornelia Knight (1758-1837) knew Johnson during her girlhood in London (all biographical information from Luttrell). Her parents' connection with Sir Joshua Reynolds and his sister Frances gave them entrée into Johnson's circle, so Cornelia grew up with the Thrales, Anna Williams, Elizabeth Montagu, Goldsmith, Burke, Boswell, and Johnson as family friends. Mrs. Knight, although she did not allow her own minimal education to handicap her in this intellectual circle, nevertheless saw to it that her daughter had an unusually thorough academic training as well as the advantages of Johnson's literary society. The Knights' London life was interrupted by three years in Plymouth (1770-73) when Cornelia's father returned briefly to active duty in the Navy and won his knighthood. But his career did not prosper, and the family returned to London. There Sir Joseph's health, already poor, declined until, in 1775, he died.

Lady Knight was then faced with a problem common among widows at the time: money. She had some small resources, but her husband had not played the political games necessary to secure a pension for her, and her family was not disposed to help. Living in

London was expensive; for a sociable woman with intellectual interests, rural retirement would be stifling. But the Continent was both culturally stimulating and relatively cheap, so in the spring of 1776, Lady Knight and Cornelia prepared to embark for France. When they said goodbye to Johnson, he warned Cornelia about the fascination of Catholicism and cautioned her not to change her religion. He may also have said, "Go, my dear, for you are too big for an island" (Luttrell, 39) – and Cornelia, then just sixteen, was in fact unusually tall. Both versions of the parting have been interpreted as planting a seed of resentment against the author of *Rasselas*.

Mother and daughter lived together on the Continent until Lady Knight's death in 1799. Part of the time was spent in France, more in Italy. Despite their comparative poverty, they moved in a society that included not only other English expatriates and Navy officers but also English and European aristocracy, and even royalty. They divided their hours between social engagements and literary and artistic pursuits. The mother apparently kept the daughter on a very short leash. Immensely proud of "my Cornelia," Lady Knight was possessive as well, regarding her as a permanent companion and, when she began to write for publication, as a possible source of additional income. Marriage or independence seem not to have been thought of. One can only guess how Cornelia felt about her situation. She wrote an autobiography (Kaye), but it is singularly unrevealing about this and many other personal matters; only rarely does Lady Knight emerge from Cornelia's narrative "we," which unites mother and daughter in apparent harmony.

After her mother's death in 1799, Miss Knight was taken into the protection of Sir William Hamilton, Ambassador to the Court of Naples, and his beautiful young wife, Emma. Admiral Horatio Nelson, about whose victories Cornelia had written glowing praise in verse, was also charged with her care. Nelson was an intimate of the Ambassador's household, and was then becoming particularly intimate with Lady Hamilton. In 1800, Miss Knight accompanied them all on a triumphal return to England where Nelson was greeted as the hero of the Nile, but she did not stay with them long to bask in his glory. Made aware, apparently belatedly, of Nelson's relationship with Emma, the morally upright Miss Knight sought other society. In 1805 she took up a vaguely defined position in the Queen's household, and later served as companion to the Princess Charlotte.

These were years of pride and pain, of high status – and hurt feelings when that status was insufficiently recognized. Nearly half of her autobiography concentrates on these nine of her nearly eighty years, the highest, and, when she was dismissed, the lowest points in her life. The elderly Miss Knight then retired to the Continent and spent her last years as she had spent her youth, among the aristocracy and minor royalty. A return to England proved unsatisfactory, and she drifted back to Italy and finally to France, where, in 1837, she died.

Ellis Cornelia Knight's literary productions were varied. Histories of Spain and France, translations of German literature, poems, prayers, and hymns took second place to four major works: *Marcus Flaminius* (1793), a novel about ancient Rome; *A Description of Latium* (1805), illustrated with her own etchings; *Sir Guy de Lusignan* (1833), an historical novel; and *Dinarbas*.

Dinarbas; A Tale: Being a Continuation of Rasselas, Prince of Abissinia (1790) was, according to Lady Knight, written to amuse her when she was ill. The author states a more public purpose in her Introduction: to delineate "the fairer prospect" of life and afford "consolation . . . to the wretched traveller" on his way through life's "rugged paths" (10). She picks up the story exactly where Johnson leaves off, and, like Johnson, debates philosophical questions. She introduces new characters and, unlike Johnson, a wealth of incident; some of the events in her sequel are specifically or generally historical, whereas *Rasselas* is comparatively timeless. And she has a conclusion, something like a happily-ever-after.

Despite its close connections with *Rasselas*, *Dinarbas* is a different kind of book – and the question of genre is of some significance for both. Critics argue over how to classify *Rasselas*, but the best label is still "apologue," that is, a fiction created to demonstrate the truth of a statement, in this case a statement about the nature of happiness. Exactly what that statement is, however, is also a matter for debate, but Knight perceived it as a claim that happiness, because it is not permanent, is not real, and that life is therefore a bleak affair. To some extent *Dinarbas* too is an apologue, but it offers a different statement about happiness, which is again matter for debate: is Johnson wrong and does *Dinarbas* refute his claim? or does the sequel not simply deny but re-view and qualify Johnson's stance?

Insofar as it is an apologue, *Dinarbas* addresses directly the same question that *Rasselas* does. But the sequel is also a novel, a new genre in the eighteenth century, and one which owes much of its development to women writers. Women often wrote novels simply to make a living, but the more usual theories for their attraction to the genre are that, being new, it did not demand the classical education that women lacked, and that, focussing on the domestic scene, it presented women with the chance to write about what they knew best. But Knight had been given an unusually good education, which included some training in the classics, and *Dinarbas* contains only a few domestic interludes among its many scenes of military action, political intrigue, exotic travel, and other adventures. More probably, then, she, and perhaps other women writers as well, chose the genre because of the opportunities it offered to portray character – to show the growth and development of the individual as events unfold and experience accumulates, the interactions of one person with another, the making and changing of relationships; concern for relationships is often said to be more characteristic of women than of men.

Character is indeed of minimal concern for Johnson in *Rasselas*. His travellers, though their shortcomings are sometimes the objects of his satire, are primarily designed to be detached observers who give voice to a range of opinion and argument about the nature of happiness and other ideas. In her Preface to *Rasselas*, Anna Laetitia Barbauld found these "insulated being[s], detached from all connexions and all duties," quite improbable, because "no man is so insulated: we are woven into the web of society" (iii). And indeed Johnson's characters are insulated: despite the experience they all acquire as they roam the world, they are unchanged at the end of Johnson's story. Knight, on the other hand, makes her travellers grow and develop. Woven into the web of society despite their high rank and privileged positions, they learn from experience, they come to understand themselves, they fall in love – they are more nearly novelistic characters than Johnson's. Her choice of genre, therefore, can be seen as part of her comment on *Rasselas* and part of her statement about the nature of happiness: Johnson's detached observers are too far removed from human involvement to have an accurate sense of the fullness of life, so his book presents an inaccurate or at least incomplete sense of the nature of happiness.

It is arguable, then, that Knight's gender influenced her decision to make *Dinarbas* not only an apologue but also a novel, in contrast to *Rasselas*, which is concerned only with "abstract questions" and depicts "life . . . viewed at a distance by a speculative man," as Barbauld says (iii, v). The argument about gender can also be extended beyond the matter of genre to other elements in the two books. It is revealing to compare not only parallel incidents like Rasselas's encounters with the young men of Cairo but also Johnson's and Knight's use of landscape, their ideas about religion and the emphasis they give to futurity, their implied political positions, their attitudes to social rank and other forms of power (and powerlessness), their senses of the individual's degree of freedom, and other points. In short, there are marked differences as well as similarities in their attitudes on the topics they share. Each book raises some issues that do not appear in the other. And yet, whether or not the reader wants to follow up the many possible comparisons, and whether he or she finds the argument based on gender valid or invalid, *Dinarbas* is well worth reading. Cornelia Knight has done a lively and entertaining job of finishing Samuel Johnson's story.

Bibliographical Note

Five editions of *Dinarbas* alone were published in England in Ellis Cornelia Knight's lifetime (1790, 1792, 1793, 1800, 1811); others were published as an additional volume of *Rasselas*, and several appeared in the United States. The first edition is the source for this reprint; it was seen through the press in London, while the author was abroad, by the translator and dramatist John Hoole, a family friend (Eliott-Drake, 136; Luttrell, 29). Original spelling and punctuation have been retained; the Errata and typographical errors have been corrected, and some inconsistencies in capitalization and punctuation have been regularized. Definitions supplied in the notes are quoted or adapted from Johnson's *Dictionary of the English Language* (1755) unless otherwise indicated.

Works Cited

Barbauld, Anna Laetitia, ed. *The British Novelists.* 50 vols. London: Rivington, 1810. Preface to Johnson's *Rasselas.*
Eliott-Drake, Lady, ed. *Lady Knight's Letters from France and Italy 1776-1795.* London: Humphreys, 1905.
Hawkins, Sir John. *The Life of Samuel Johnson, LL.D.* (1787). Ed. Bertram H. Davis. London: Cape, 1962.
Kaye, J. W., ed. *Autobiography of Miss Cornelia Knight, Lady Companion to the Princess Charlotte of Wales.* 2 vols. London: Allen, 1861.
Knight, Ellis Cornelia. *Dinarbas; A Tale: Being a Continuation of Rasselas, Prince of Abissinia.* London: Dilly, 1790.
Luttrell, Barbara. *The Prim Romantic: A Biography of Ellis Cornelia Knight.* London: Chatto and Windus, 1965.

Suggestions for Further Reading

Messenger, Ann. "Choices of Life: Samuel Johnson and Ellis Cornelia Knight." In *His and Hers: Essays in Restoration and Eighteenth-Century Literature.* Lexington: University Press of Kentucky, 1986, 197-221.
Rawson, C. J. "The Continuation of *Rasselas.*" In *Bicentenary Essays on "Rasselas,"* ed. Magdi Wahba. Cairo: S.O.P. Press, 1959, 85-95.
Uphaus, Robert W. "Cornelia Knight's *Dinarbas*: A Sequel to *Rasselas,*" *Philological Quarterly* 65 (1986): 433-46.

DINARBAS;
A TALE:

BEING A CONTINUATION OF

RASSELAS, Prince of Abissinia

Rectius occupat
Nomen beati, qui Deorum
Muneribus sapienter uti,
Duramque callet pauperiem pati,
Pejusque letho flagitium timet:
Non ille pro caris amicis,
Aut patria timidus perire.
Hor. Lib. iv. Od. 9.

(Horace, Ode 4:9 ". . . far better does he claim the name of 'happy man' who knows to use with wisdom heaven's gifts, and how to bear the pinch of poverty; who dreads dishonor more than death, who's not afraid to die for well-loved friends and fatherland." A.H. Bryce, trans.)

INTRODUCTION

BY AN IRREVOCABLE law of the state, all the sons and daughters of the royal house of Abissinia were decreed to pass their days in a delightful retreat, named the happy valley, except such as were, from time to time, called by the order of succession to the throne. Rasselas, the emperor's fourth son, weary of being secluded from the world, makes his escape by the assistance of Imlac, a poet and philosopher, and visits Egypt, accompanied by his favourite sister Nekayah, and her attendant Pekuah. They examine different stations and professions of men, and contract a friendship with an astronomer, possessed of deep science and an excellent heart, but who had fallen into a species of visionary madness, by which he was led to imagine himself endued with a power to regulate and distribute the various seasons of the year, and changes of the weather, till his intercourse with the travellers dissipates this mental delusion. After many fruitless enquiries in search of a life of happiness, Rasselas and Nekayah, with their companions and the astronomer, resolve to return to the happy valley.

Such is the general plan of the inimitable tale of *Rasselas Prince of Abissinia*, written by the late Dr. Johnson, which it has been thought necessary to prefix as an introduction to the following work.

Sir John Hawkins, in his life of Dr. Johnson, says, "that the writer had an intention of marrying his hero, and placing him in a state of permanent felicity." This passage suggested the idea of the continuation now offered, with the greatest diffidence, to the reader, and without any thought of a vain and presumptuous comparison; as every attempt to imitate the energetic stile, strong imagery, and profound knowledge, of the author of *Rasselas*, would be equally rash with that of the suitors to bend the bow of Ulysses.[1]

---

[1] In Homer's *Odyssey*, only Ulysses was strong enough to bend his own bow, although the suitors besieging his wife Penelope tried to when she challenged them. Knight's modesty here is characteristic of introductions to eighteenth-century women's books.

It is indeed much to be regretted, that the same pencil[2] which so forcibly painted the evils attendant on humanity, had not delineated the fairer prospect. That such a prospect exists, will scarcely be denied; and if the narrative of *Dinarbas*, however defective, shall be found to afford any consolation or relief to the wretched traveller, terrified and disheartened at the rugged paths of life, this reflection will compensate the want of genius and literary fame of its author, who, under the veil of concealment,[3] anxiously awaits the judgment of the critic, not wholly without ambition to merit the favour and indulgence of a candid[4] Public.

---

[2]*pencil*: "A small brush of hair which painters dip in their colours."
[3]*Dinarbas* was published anonymously.
[4]*candid*: "Without malice, fair."

CONTENTS

1. Reflections on the return to the happy valley......................13
2. The prince is no longer left to his own choice.....................16
3. The prince embraces a new state of life.............................19
4. Rasselas acquires a friend..22
5. The fortress besieged..25
6. The princess meets with a real misfortune........................29
7. The love of dissipation not incorrigible............................31
8. Apology for rusticity..34
9. Rasselas in confinement..37
10. The resources of solitude...39
11. Resignation...41
12. Nekayah instructed by misfortune...............................43
13. The funeral of Dinarbas...46
14. Embarrassment of Nekayah.....................................49
15. Dinarbas justifies the confidence of the princess..................52
16. Advantages and disadvantages of the sacerdotal station..........54
17. Danger of fanaticism...57
18. Troubles in Abissinia...60
19. The same subject continued......................................62
20. The prince gives proof of real courage...........................64
21. The prince returns to the fortress................................66
22. The power of artifice..69
23. Rasselas endeavours to produce a reconciliation.................71
24. Victory and gratitude to the conqueror..........................74
25. Retrospect of a life of dissipation................................76
26. A new inhabitant enters the valley..............................80
27. Return of a friend...83
28. Adventures of Dinarbas...85
29. Adventures of Dinarbas continued..............................87
30. Dinarbas visits the emperor.......................................89
31. Sketch of the travels of Dinarbas................................92
32. Grandeur of the ancients..95
33. The prince and princess accompany their father to Gonthar.....98
34. Inconveniences of foreign aid....................................100

35. Death of the emperor..103
36. Reflections of Rasselas on his accession to the throne..........105
37. Letter of Zilia...107
38. Amalphis accepts the command of the troops.....................109
39. Rasselas takes a view of the legislature of Abissinia............111
40. Priests at court..114
41. History of Elphenor..116
42. The utility of learning...118
43. The same subject continued..120
44. Education..123
45. False pretensions to knowledge....................................126
46. The conversation turns on various matters.......................128
47. Simplicity..131
48. Dinarbas returns from the court of the sultan....................134
49. Marriages of Rasselas and Nekayah..............................136
50. Visit to the happy valley..138

Chapter 1

REFLECTIONS ON THE RETURN TO THE HAPPY VALLEY

THE INUNDATION having subsided, the prince and princess with their companions left Cairo, and proceeded on their way to Abissinia: the journey was long and tedious, and their reflections on their return were by no means satisfactory.

"Are we then," said Rasselas, "no wiser than when we set out; or have we only learned, that all enquiries after happiness are vain, and that a state of mere vegetation is the highest degree of felicity which mortals are permitted to obtain in this world?"

"We have, at least," answered the princess, "acquired sufficient knowledge to instruct those whom we formerly left behind, and whom we are now going to rejoin:[5] we may convince them by our experience of the fallacy of human enjoyments; we may guard them against the delusive powers of imagination, and teach them to be contented with that state which, by our example, they will find preferable to the several occupations of life."

"Not only this," said Pekuah, "but we shall add to their amusements the relation of the various scenes we have met with on our travels: our conversation will be sought for, because we can instruct and entertain; and while we renew our past pleasures by relating them, sheltered from the storms of life, the memory of the dangers we have escaped, and the hardships we have undergone, will give a higher relish to our state of security."

"How we may be received by the inhabitants of the happy valley," replied the prince, "or how we may be entertained by our own reflections, is to me uncertain. I wish[6] we may not be more discontented with the valley than we were while unacquainted with other scenes: wandering has often given a momentary desire of settled residence; but activity is natural to man, and he who has once tasted

---

[5]*Rasselas* ends with the decision to return to Abissinia, but nothing is said about going back to the happy valley.
[6]*wish*: "To have strong desire"; "It has a slight signification of hope."

the joys of liberty and action will no more be contented with perpetual rest and seclusion, than he, who may have wished for sleep in a moment of lassitude, would desire to remain inactive on his couch, after the light of the sun has awakened him from oblivion and repose. I am, however, neither displeased with our past attempts, nor hopeless for our future success: as we advance in years the fire of imagination will cool, and the agitation of restlessness subside: we have laid up a stock of knowledge which will teach us to distinguish real merit from false pretension. Reason, whom we have already perceived from afar, advances towards us as youth recedes, and I doubt not but, by taking her for our guide, we shall enjoy that serenity, calmness, and justness of perception, which are alone worthy of a thinking being."

"Far be it from me, Sir," said Imlac, "to anticipate your disappointment, or to increase your alarms; yet permit me to tell you that eminent knowledge, if not accompanied with singular indulgence to others, often serves to render its possessors miserable, nay even ridiculous: your experience and your studies have placed you in a class of beings, very different from the inhabitants of the happy valley, whom you can only treat with condescension or with contempt. Society can not subsist without equality, and while you are considered as a prince, and as a man of superior intelligence, you may command admiration, but you can not ensure affection."

"Alas!" said the astronomer, "if reason is a blessing, it has the same fate as patience; we never invoke it until we have been fatigued with the rapturous wanderings of imagination, and exhausted by the exquisite feelings of sensibility;[7] we then apply to reason as a refuge from care; it convinces without persuading, it instructs without improving us: reason should regulate, but a warmer motive must inspire our actions: devotion and benevolence, the two noblest incitements to virtue, are emanations of the heart, not reflections of the head; reason may come to their support, but has not the merit of creating them. Our condition in this world is too distant from perfection to give us hopes of enjoying any one advantage in the supreme degree: for the experience of age, we must resign the gaiety of youth: we must sacrifice heroism to prudence, genius to

---

[7]*sensibility*: capacity for refined emotion; readiness to feel compassion and to be moved by the pathetic in literature and art (OED).

correctness, and rapture to tranquillity: these are called the victories of reason, but I confess I rather attribute them to the influence of time. The wise man, in resignation to the decrees of Providence, repines not at the loss of the advantages of youth, and rejoices in the consolations granted to old age; but we know of none, either wise or foolish, who would voluntarily relinquish those pleasures, which are peculiar to the spring and summer of his days, to anticipate the hour when he must in vain look back on what he has neglected to enjoy."

Chapter 2

THE PRINCE IS NO LONGER LEFT TO HIS OWN CHOICE

RASSELAS, NOTWITHSTANDING his doubts, was resolved to continue his journey: he reached the confines of Abissinia without accident, where, as he was discoursing with his sister on what methods they should take to excuse their absence when they arrived at the happy valley, their caravan was stopped by several horsemen of the king's troops, headed by a youth of animated countenance and courteous manners. "Strangers," said he, "you are perhaps ignorant of the orders we have received. The Egyptians have lately committed hostilities on the Abissinian territories, and we can not permit any of that nation to pass our boundaries: tell me therefore what is your country, and what the motive of your travels?"

"Sir," replied the prince, "we are travellers from curiosity, and our native country is Abissinia: you may therefore suffer us freely to enter into the dominions of your powerful monarch, and, if you please, we will remain under your guard till we have obtained from the court permission to continue our journey: we are not unknown there, and I have no doubt but our request will be speedily granted."

The young warrior, well pleased with the answer of Rasselas, conducted him, and his companions, to a fortress on the banks of the river that separates Abissinia from Egypt.

The governor of this fortress, whose name was Amalphis, was a man of lofty stature and majestic presence; his hair was white as silver, his eyes were piercing as the mid-day sun, and several scars imprinted on his venerable countenance were the honourable testimonies of his service. He received the prince and ladies with urbanity; and with a look of penetrative enquiry demanded the motive of their journey. His son Dinarbas, the young warrior who had conducted them to the fort, repeated what Rasselas had told him.

"The motive of curiosity," replied Amalphis, "though laudable, is so uncommon in this country, that we cannot, without injustice to ourselves and detriment to our emperor's service, permit you to proceed on your journey, till the return of your messenger from the capital: in the mean time we expect you to give an account of your names, families and peregrination."

The prince, not choosing to declare his name and quality, left to Imlac the care of answering the questions of the governor. The poet, without departing from truth, concealed as much as prudence required: he told Amalphis that he was Imlac the merchant, who had resided some time at Cairo in the occupations of commerce, that he had been accompanied thither by this young man and his sister, who were Abissinians of rank, and had a desire to see the world and make choice of the state of life most conducive to happiness; that finding equal disappointment in all, they were now resolved to return to their former dwelling, and pass the remainder of their lives in study and contemplation.

"As for myself," said the astronomer, "I will freely confess that I am by birth an Egyptian and an inhabitant of Cairo; but my life has been spent in the pursuits of knowledge and in the labyrinths of science: whoever has assisted me in my endeavours, has been my countryman: the world is my school, and its inhabitants my fellow students: my disquisitions tend not towards the welfare or ruin of any particular state: if my studies could be of any utility, I would not confine their influence to one spot of the habitable globe. If truth and wisdom are emanations of the divine Spirit, surely their benefits ought to be generally distributed amongst our fellow-creatures: whatever regard I have for my own country, my way of life has made me consider myself as a citizen of the universe, or rather I have considered only my studies; and my mind, busied with intellectual enjoyments, has been equally uninterested in the shock of great empires and the petty pursuits of domestic life. I have lately known blessings of which I was before ignorant – the charms of society and the consolations of friendship – deprive me not of these, O governor! permit me to remain with persons who honour me with their confidence, and console me with their benevolence; and be assured, that I have neither the power nor the inclination to change any thing in the fate of empires."

Amalphis was willing to believe the ingenuous declaration of the astronomer. Imlac and the prince seemed mysterious, but their train being neither sufficiently numerous to announce open force, nor small enough to give the suspicion of hidden treachery, he desired Imlac to dispatch his messenger, and in the mean time assigned the company an apartment in his castle, where he treated them with the respect due to their appearance, and often questioned them on their travels, the different incidents of which they willingly related.

"I am amazed," said Amalphis, "how you should have ever imagined that happiness depended on any particular station in life. Providence indeed has permitted to a very few the choice of the path which they are to take in this world: the lower class of citizens are generally debarred by poverty from following the dictates of their inclination, and the great are still more irresistibly restrained by the prejudice of custom: those few, who have it in their power to choose, are too often guided by their passions: it remains therefore equally for him who has been compelled into any state of life by the will of others, and for him who has been so by the force of his own imagination, to do his duty with firmness and resignation, whatever may be his disgust or repentance. There is no profession in which a man may not be virtuous and respected: the fault lies not in the state of life, it depends on the manner of acting: a man who is discontented with his employment, and for that reason neglects his duties, shews both want of sense and want of courage: if he acts up to the part allotted him, at least he fills some character in life: if he abandons it because it is contrary to his inclination, he either does nothing, or goes out of his sphere; his existence is therefore useless. On the other hand, the priest who repines at consecrating his days to meditation or pastoral instruction, who wishes for the active life of a soldier and is fired with enthusiasm when he hears the trumpet sound to arms, has more merit than his companions if he only feels these sentiments internally, and employs the energy that Heaven has given him to conquer his repugnance, and to be more active in his functions. The soldier who would have wished to pass his days in literary ease and philosophical disquisition, yet, far from neglecting his duty to his king and country, makes his studies serve to the perfection of the art of war, is a greater hero than he whom the desire alone of military fame drives headlong to the field. Similar examples may be found in any condition, and he alone is wretched and contemptible, who will not act at least with decency, if not with distinction, the part assigned him on this great theatre. Courage, though a virtue peculiarly essential to our profession, is necessary in all: it teaches us equally to act with glory, and to suffer with patience: it inspires us with firmness towards men, and resignation towards God."

Chapter 3

THE PRINCE EMBRACES A NEW STATE OF LIFE

IT WAS EXPECTED that some time might elapse before the return of the messenger dispatched to the court of Abissinia, and in the mean while the prince told Imlac that he had an inclination to propose to the governor making an expedition with his son.

"I have always," said he, "felt a desire for the military life; my passion for glory was roused in the happy valley by the theory of the art of war, which the most skilful masters are ordered to instil into us, from the possibility that we may one day be obliged to act as commanders of a great army. I have often wished to put these lessons in practice; and surely any employment would be preferable to the state of inactivity, in which we are doomed to remain till the return of our messenger."

"Sir," answered Imlac, "if you persist in this intention, I will accompany you with pleasure: a camp is no unfavourable study for a poet: but let me first warn you of one thing, which has probably escaped your reflection: you are accustomed to command, and totally unacquainted with the subordination of a military life: constraint and obedience are equally unknown to you, and yet you will be obliged to execute every order of Dinarbas like the meanest of his soldiers."

"I know not," replied the prince, "whether such a life would be agreeable to me for a long duration; but one campaign can not exhaust my patience: all evils of which we may calculate the term, are at least to be endured; and why should not I contentedly submit to a life which so many rejoice in?"

"As for me, Sir," said the astronomer, "you will forgive me if I do not accompany you; my age requires tranquillity, and my country forbids me to bear arms against her: I will stay with the princess and Pekuah."

Nekayah entered in the midst of this conversation: she was far from approving the prince's intentions; she dreaded being left among persons to whom she was unknown; she represented to her brother that a son of the emperor was not to hazard his life like the meanest of his subjects, and that slaves were made to defend their master.

"Sister," said the prince, "I blush to hear a reasoning so contrary to the principles of duty and humanity – who is to defend the father, if not the son? And what right have princes to expect the assistance of their subjects if they will not join in bearing a part of the toil? What obligations can the governor of this fortress and his son have to my father, in comparison with those I owe him? Indeed to speak frankly, I see not why my life is more precious than that of Amalphis: he has served the emperor during several years; his loss would be felt on these frontiers: the enemy might gain ground and the peace of Abissinia be endangered: his death would introduce despair into his now happy family: his son would be left at the most dangerous period of life without the counsels of a wise and prudent father; his daughter, in the bloom of youth and beauty, would remain friendless and unprotected. Where would be the fatal consequences of my fall? The importance of those who fill exalted stations is often imaginary, and what appears great in the eyes of the possessor is perhaps totally indifferent to others. I would have thee divest thyself, Nekayah, of every prejudice of this nature, and seriously consider that no man is really important, but as he is useful to his country."

The arrival of Dinarbas put an end to this discourse; he learned and applauded the resolution of Rasselas, and offered him his friendship with all the warmth natural to his age and profession.

Rasselas had another motive for his departure besides those he had mentioned to Imlac and the princess. Zilia the daughter of Amalphis appeared to him entirely different from the women he had known in the happy valley, or during his travels: the first were slaves, the others lost the power in the attempt to please: Zilia seemed unconscious of her charms; her mind was cultivated by her father with assiduous care; her sentiments, naturally liberal, had received from education the dignity of superior virtue: she neither avoided nor sought the conversation of the strangers; yet all were interested by her.

Rasselas however, though he had acquired much philosophy by his reading and observation, still retained the idea that women, if not beings of an inferior class, were at least not worthy of gaining too great an ascendancy over the minds of men: he knew his own sensibility, and feared lest he should become the slave of a passion, which he despised as trivial, or censured as romantic;[8] he therefore hoped a short absence would obliterate the impression which he began to perceive Zilia had made on him, and seriously resolved to drive from his mind all thoughts of her till his return. Time, which while considered as future always promises happiness and wisdom, would, he doubted not, destroy the power of this enchantment: he therefore hastened the departure of Dinarbas, and they sallied forth, at the head of fifty horse, to make an incursion on the enemy's frontiers.

---

[8]*romantic*: "Resembling the tales of romances; wild"; "Fanciful."

Chapter 4

RASSELAS ACQUIRES A FRIEND

AFTER AN ABSENCE of a few weeks Rasselas and Dinarbas returned triumphant with the spoils of many conquered enemies: their friendship had been cemented by mutual testimonies of valour and of kindness, and the prince was surprised to see how much this expedition had raised him in the esteem of Amalphis, his son, and Zilia.

"You are now," said the old warrior, "our friend and fellow-soldier; you have proved your fidelity to your king and country, and we need not fear to treat you with that confidence, with which your ingenuous and open manner at first inspired us."

Imlac, whom the prince had not permitted to accompany him, that he might remain with Nekayah, could not forbear remarking the new esteem which Rasselas had acquired with the inhabitants of the fortress.

"Prince," said he, "how necessary is general knowledge to a man of your exalted station! Of what avail had been in this citadel your literature and philosophy, if your activity and courage had not added to these endowments the honours of military service? He who is useful will always be respected: in the moments of repose and tranquillity we are pleased with the man who can instruct or amuse us; but, in the hour of distress and danger, we neglect him if he cannot be essentially useful."

Nekayah complained much to her brother of the time in which he had been absent; "She was weary," she said, "of seeing every day the same faces, and hearing the same discourses; the conversation of Amalphis was indeed instructive and entertaining, but he was great part of the day engrossed by his duty; and Zilia, though kind and gentle in her manners, did not treat her with that respect which the distance between them might naturally have inspired her with." "Can you blame," replied the prince, "the daughter of Amalphis for denying respect to that rank which you industriously conceal, and of which she can have no idea? You hide from others, but cannot yourself forget, that you are a princess; lose this idea for a moment, and you will find in the society of Zilia the same pleasure which I feel in that of her brother. I am delighted with the familiarity of Dinarbas; he believes himself my equal, and I am flattered with having, for the first time in my life, excited disinterested regard; which I suppose granted either to the qualities implanted in me by nature, or to those which I may have acquired by my own industry. I am pleased with the vivacity of his temper, and the energy of his mind: I am resolved to make another expedition with him, and endeavour to confirm the good opinion he has conceived of me."

Notwithstanding the wise resolutions of Rasselas, he found in the conversation and manners of Zilia an irresistible charm; he began now to condemn his former opinions as unjust and illiberal. "What greater happiness," said he to himself, "could I experience than in passing my life with a being endowed with such perfection, and who feels so little her own superiority! But shall I have the power of choosing for myself? Am I not doomed to be for ever the victim of state and prejudice, and shall I disturb the heavenly serenity of Zilia by seeking to inspire her with sentiments, which can only render her as miserable as myself!"

Dinarbas found the prince absorbed in meditation. "My friend," said he, "I am grieved to see you pensive and unhappy: were it in our power to restore you to liberty, you should not languish in confinement; yet how often shall I regret the moments we have passed together! with what difficulty shall I tear myself from Nekayah! You think me not sufficiently deserving of your confidence to disclose to me the secret of your birth, and of the rank you held in Abissinia; I have reason to believe it elevated, both from your sentiments, from those of Nekayah, and from the respect with which you are treated by your fellow travellers: you may perhaps be offended at my frankness, when I tell you it would have been more fortunate for me if I had never known your sister: with the gentlest manners and the most engaging urbanity, she has sometimes a haughtiness that would lessen considerably any other woman in my esteem, and yet she possesses the power of making me instantaneously forget the distance which she had seemed to prescribe me, whenever the natural sweetness of her temper breaks through the constraint which she imposes on herself and others."

"Dinarbas!" interrupted the prince, "in the name of our friendship, let us drop this subject; if thou couldst see into my heart, thou wouldst find me unhappy as thyself – let us depart with the next dawn, and attack the enemies of our country."

Chapter 5

THE FORTRESS BESIEGED

WHILE THE TWO friends were engaged in this conversation, Amalphis, having received intelligence that a large body of Egyptians and Arabs was advancing to assault the fortress, commanded his son to delay his intended expedition till he could be certain of the truth of this information. In the mean time he took every necessary precaution to prevent the enemy from finding him unprepared; he doubled the guard on the walls, went round every night to see that all was in order, and assigned to every soldier the post he was to defend.

The princess could not without some uneasiness behold these preparatives for war, and Pekuah was greatly alarmed: the prince comforted them by assurances of security, of which, however, he was perhaps no more persuaded than they; yet his consolations, given with an air of confidence, had the desired effect, and the ladies accustomed themselves to the expectation of a siege, with as little concern as if they had never apprehended it. During this interval of uncertainty, the prince was neither able, nor indeed desirous, to avoid the company of Zilia; but he soon found her greatly altered; her anxieties returned, and she could not consider the danger, to which Amalphis was soon to be exposed, without the greatest uneasiness. In vain did she endeavour to assume her usual gaiety in her father's presence: in the midst of a lively conversation she would often burst into tears, and every night, when she bade adieu to Amalphis and her brother, she embraced them with an impression of sorrow in her countenance, which she vainly endeavoured to conceal.

Rasselas was deeply affected with the grief of Zilia; he could not refrain from telling her he had observed it, nor avoid expressing the pain it gave him: she received his consolations with sensibility, and treated him with more consideration than ever.

The princess was less pleased with the conduct of Dinarbas: since the day of his conversation with Rasselas, he had sought to disengage himself from the pleasure he found in listening to her, he studiously avoided Nekayah, and discoursed only with Pekuah. The favourite thoughtlessly encouraged his advances, and the pride of Nekayah was mortified: she found every day less delight in the company of her dear Pekuah, she took every opportunity of separating herself from one whose absence had formerly made her resolve to abandon the world, and without whom she had considered existence as a torment;[9] yet would she often reproach herself for this change of sentiments. Pekuah had still the same tender respect, the same attachment for the princess which had been the greatest happiness of her life: Nekayah could only accuse her of passing too much time with Dinarbas, and she had herself found too great a pleasure in his company to condemn another for seeking it. She felt that jealousy was the motive of her new and extraordinary dislike; her pride and her principles equally combated this passion; she was surprised to find it possible that she could be susceptible of it; and was ashamed to listen to the voice that internally accused her.

While her mind was in this agitation she one morning observed a great dust arising in the east: a general tumult in the fortress soon convinced her, that she had not been the only person who had remarked it. "The army of the Egyptians is advancing to attack us," said Dinarbas, who at that instant entered her apartment, "yet be not alarmed, Nekayah! you are here in safety, and did you know our hearts, you would be convinced that we would either defend you or perish: our numbers are not contemptible, and our courage has been often tried: the enemy's troops are numerous, but ours are better disciplined, and my father is no young soldier."

"Dinarbas!" answered the princess, "I thank you for your care; I have not the resolution of a warrior, but I am resigned: the first appearance of danger naturally alarms the mind of woman; but give me time for reflection, and I am prepared for all – your duty is to repulse the enemy, ours to pray for your success, and to await the event with patience."

Dinarbas hastened to his post, and the princess remained on a sofa in silent and anxious expectation. She had not been long in this situation before she was joined by Pekuah, who throwing herself at the feet of her mistress embraced her knees with a flood of tears: "Dear lady," said she, "this is the most cruel moment of my life:

---

[9]See *Rasselas*, chapters 34-35.

when I was taken by the Arabs, I consoled myself with the reflection that you did not share my misfortunes: alas! I am now doomed to see the princess of Abissinia in the power of lawless robbers, and the sacred person of the prince exposed to their savage fury – what fatal stars conducted us to this fortress!"

"Pekuah!" answered the princess, calmly, "a few days since you seemed to consider this fortress as the habitation of your choice; joy animated your eyes, and inspired your tongue; all your sentiments, even your attachment to me, seemed absorbed in the delights of society, and I have reason to believe that your present fears arise more from the danger of losing that society, than from the perils to which the prince or myself may be exposed."

"Beloved mistress," replied Pekuah, "if you withdraw your favour from your slave, she can only bow her head beneath your displeasure, and sink into her original state of insignificancy – but wherein can Nekayah accuse me of forgetting that respectful tenderness which alone possesses my heart? I am not conscious of any change of manners, or how that vivacity, which formerly used to meet your approbation in our discourses with Imlac and the astronomer, can have displeased you in this fortress; where, from the want of variety of objects, you allowed it was necessary to snatch every occasional amusement, and avail ourselves of every trivial matter that could excite it."

"But why," resumed the princess, a little softened, "would you spend so much of your time with the son of Amalphis? Though your understanding and your virtue place you above the malignity of slander, why should you peculiarly choose the conversation of this young warrior in preference to the sage discourse of his father, or the lively and instructive converse of Imlac and the astronomer?"

"I know not, lady," answered Pekuah, "that I have held more discourse with Dinarbas than with the other inhabitants of the fortress; but if you command it, I will henceforward avoid his company, nor shall I consider it as a sacrifice to my obedience; indeed," added she, smiling, "if Nekayah will allow me to proceed without being offended at her servant, I will confess to her that I find not in the society of Dinarbas those charms which so warmly affect the prince and Imlac: in the midst of the most interesting conversation his thoughts often wander from the subject, and his eyes are turned on Nekayah. I am fully conscious of the infinite attractions of my princess, and I cannot sometimes avoid pitying the youth for having nourished aspiring sentiments, of the vanity of which he is, perhaps, unconscious, and which yet his respect endeavours to stifle: but surely no woman can entirely conquer the pride inherent in our sex, nor likes to be the senseless idol that is crowned with flowers, while the vows and incense are offered to the Divinity."

The princess felt the truth of her favourite's discourse, and, at the same instant, found all her affection for her revive; but great were the accusations with which she loaded herself: she regretted her blindness, and at the same time upbraided her own heart for the pleasure which the discovery of Pekuah had given her: she anxiously prayed for the return of the messenger, that she might depart, and, if possible, lose the memory of all that had interested her in the castle.

Chapter 6

THE PRINCESS MEETS WITH A REAL MISFORTUNE

NEKAYAH HAD never before found herself in so uneasy a situation: her eyes were fixed on the ground, and she knew not what answer to make to Pekuah, when they were suddenly interrupted by the arrival of Zilia, who wild with grief entered the apartment, and uttering a heart-piercing shriek sunk lifeless on the ground. Pekuah ran hastily to her assistance, but Nekayah was unable to move; she raised her eyes to heaven and remained in motionless horror; she dreaded to learn the cause of Zilia's affliction; a thousand confused images took possession of her mind, and the idea of Rasselas and Dinarbas rushed at once on her imagination.

The assistance of Pekuah soon recovered the unhappy Zilia. "Nekayah!" cried she, "I have cruel tidings to relate, but your misfortune is less than mine; your brother remains a prisoner among the Egyptians, but Dinarbas has scarcely a moment to live – even now perhaps he expires, and I have lost the only poor consolation of receiving his last breath. – I saw him covered with wounds and in a state of insensibility – his valour and that of your brother have saved the fortress, but they are victims to our safety – the enemy has retired with great loss – Yet why should I repine? – Gracious Heaven!" continued she, falling on her knees, "thou art merciful; my father lives, though he lives to misery – his laurels cost him the life of his beloved son, and he has no comfort left but the wretched Zilia – let me haste to find him, and by my tender cares endeavour to calm the sorrow that overwhelms him – I forget – he commands me to remain here, and will not suffer me to be witness of the mournful scene."

At this moment Imlac appeared, and confirmed the dreadful truth: he conjured Nekayah to take comfort, but she remained the image of despair, and returned no answer either to him or Pekuah; at length, casting her eyes on Zilia, she embraced her and shed a torrent of tears.

She seemed now a little relieved, and listened with attention to the narrative of Imlac, who told her that Amalphis had received with determined valour the assault of the enemy, many of whom had scaled the walls and entered the fortress; but that after a severe conflict they fled, and were pursued by Dinarbas and Rasselas at the head of their horsemen; that when they came to the plain beneath the castle, the enemy turned and renewed the combat with desperate fury; that the two young warriors fought with distinguished courage, till Dinarbas, pierced with wounds, fell lifeless from his horse, and was carried from the field by his soldiers, who fled with him to the fortress; and Rasselas, engaged in the midst of the enemy's troops, was at the same instant surrounded and taken prisoner: "You have much cause for comfort, lady," continued Imlac, "your brother's life is in safety, the Egyptians are not a cruel nation, and it is not probable they will treat injuriously a prisoner of war."

"I thank Heaven," returned the princess, "for having protected the life of my brother; but can I enjoy comfort while he remains a prisoner, and while I behold the affliction of Zilia and her father? Let us seek the good Amalphis, nor leave him longer alone a prey to his sorrows."

Chapter 7

THE LOVE OF DISSIPATION NOT INCORRIGIBLE

WHILE GRIEF had thus taken possession of the victors, the routed forces of the Egyptians retired tumultuously towards the confines of their kingdom. Rasselas had too much fortitude and philosophy to be dejected or surprised at what he knew to be the common chance of war: he rejoiced at the retreat of the enemy, and submitted with patience to his fate, though he regretted that he could not share the honours of the conquerors: he had been too active in the engagement to perceive the fall of Dinarbas, but he feared some ill accident might have attended him, as he knew not otherwise how to account for losing sight of him, and for the desertion of his troops. He was strictly secured in the midst of four horsemen, during the time of their march, and at night placed in a tent surrounded by a strong guard. As soon as the army arrived in lower Egypt, he enjoyed greater liberty, and was permitted to converse with the officers; amongst whom he recognized several of the young men with whom he had been intimate at his first arrival at Cairo.[10] They received him with joy, for they had equally forgotten the abrupt manner in which he had quitted their society, and the good admonitions he had left with them. Rasselas was displeased at meeting them: "What shall I do," said he to himself, "in a society of which I have proved the inconveniences, and have felt the disgust? If I could not bear the noisy mirth, and thoughtless vivacity of my young companions, at my first entering into the various scenes of life, how shall I support the fatigue of their company when every day has increased my disapprobation of their conduct, and convinced me of the insufficiency of their amusements?"

In consequence of these reflections, he thanked them coolly for their civilities, and avoided any further intercourse with them: but the mind oppressed with cares, and accustomed to communicate its inquietudes, requires the usual relief: he found, not without

---

[10]See *Rasselas*, chapter 17.

humiliation, that some society was necessary, and that trifling as their conversation formerly appeared to him, he was compelled frequently to fly to it, as to a refuge from his own thoughts. He began to discern, in the midst of frantic gaiety and remorseless dissipation, sparks of honour, sincerity and good-nature, that were not to be stifled by the influence of passion: he pitied and esteemed the possessors of these virtues; and, having found by experience that severe rebuke and the air of superior prudence produced an effect contrary to his wishes, he took gentler and more successful means. By applauding their ardour, he taught them to distinguish courage from temerity, a sense of honour and the pride of virtue from revenge and vanity, generosity from prodigality, and friendship from blind affection: he learned, by studying their various dispositions and characters, that of the number whom he had considered as generally depraved, few were incapable of being reclaimed: and that he had judged too severely of the rest from the faults of their companions. He found that the same admonitions which they had rejected with derision, when given with the severity of a preceptor, they received with avidity when offered with the familiar kindness of a friend: by commending them for whatever he discovered praiseworthy in their conduct, and by joining in such of their pleasures as were innocent, he acquired the right of censuring their faults, and refusing to imitate their irregularities: their minds, unaccustomed to occupation, could with difficulty be brought to serious studies; but the love of novelty first engaged them to listen to Rasselas, when he proposed any improvement that had the appearance of pleasure; and the natural empire[11] of calm and rational amusements made them at last adopt from conviction what they had at first taken up through caprice. Even those who had before seemed incorrigible, gave way, either to the force of reason, or to the prevalence of example, and either insensibly joined in the reformation, or complied with what they saw the greater number approve.

    Rasselas could not, without a mixture of pleasure and regret, behold this change, which he would never have had the patience to effectuate, if he had not been compelled to it by his situation. "Why did I not, while at Cairo," thought he, "use the same methods and

---

[11]*empire*: "Supreme dominion; sovereign command."

obtain the same success? I fear I must consider myself as guilty of the irregularities of my companions during the space of time which has passed since we parted. He, who would wish to reform his fellow creatures, must study attentively the human heart: he must treat with tenderness the man whom weakness, not perverseness, has caused to deviate from the path of virtue: he must fortify by degrees his returning energy, nor dazzle at once the eyes of error with all the splendor of severe truth: he must shew her to him first under the form of compassion, of benevolence, of indulgence: innocence alone can bear the light of her unveiled majesty; repentance would sink into despair without the balm of mercy. – No, henceforward let me avoid the pride of reproof and the frown of disapprobation: let me endeavour to instruct by example, and persuade by kindness!"

Chapter 8

APOLOGY FOR RUSTICITY

WHEREVER THE ARMY passed, the prince observed that great cordiality subsisted between the soldiers and the inhabitants of the country: the former received presents of the fruits of the earth and of the milk of the flocks, which made the only riches of their rural friends. Rasselas was surprised to find great acuteness and penetration in many of these shepherds, who gave useful instructions to the soldiers for the remainder of their march, and amused them with pastoral sports, while they received them with frankness and hospitality. "How different do I find you," said Rasselas to one of the old shepherds, "from the race who tend their flocks near the cataracts of the Nile! I visited these in hopes to find amongst them that gentleness and those harmless virtues which all ages and all nations have agreed to attribute to the pastoral life. My disappointment was great; they were discontented with their own situation, envious of the rich, rude and untaught in the arts of general utility, and not more uninstructed in the politeness of courts, than in the common duties of hospitality.[12] I find, on the contrary, amongst you, many who convince me that the poets have written after nature; and I am delighted to perceive that the tranquil happiness of a pastoral life, though not universal, is not wholly banished from the earth."

"Sir," replied the shepherd, "I have in my youth passed some time in the fruitful pastures which you mention, and either the warmth of fancy, not uncommon to our nation, particularly in the spring of life, has deceived me, or the shepherds who inhabit that happy climate are endowed with the same penetration, and exercise the same hospitality as you find amongst us: nay, I have thought that they possessed these qualities in a higher degree: the purity of the air, the beautiful verdure of the fields, the infinite variety of birds that inhabit the groves on the borders of the father of waters; all these images of the power and

---

[12] See *Rasselas*, chapter 19.

goodness of the Deity must expand their hearts, and purify them from the dross of those vile passions which you describe. But, Sir, the peasant feels, and therefore may justly groan under, the pressure of the tyranny of the great: your appearance persuades me that your rank is above the class of mediocrity;[13] they have been accustomed to look on such persons as their tyrants, by whom they are never to be visited, but when they are to contribute to enrich them by the fruits of their labours, or perhaps to amuse a moment of caprice or listlessness by exciting in them sentiments of ridicule. What ideas can these have in common with the rich? If you would know their opinions and manners, you must divest yourself of the superiority which your rank has given you, and live like them. I will not promise you that such intercourse will make you amends for the sacrifice: I will only say, and your present observations may confirm it, that the poetical descriptions of pastoral life, though perhaps embellished, are not wholly fabulous; and that were you obliged to descend to our humble station, you would find our candour[14] and simplicity not unworthy of your regard. The soldier who respects our property deserves our affection, and we let him reap the fruits of his moderation and of our gratitude: we envy not his riches; if he has any, they are acquired by greater hardships than we are accustomed to, and without him we could not possess our fields in tranquillity. Blame us not therefore for our rudeness towards the mighty; it is perhaps our greatest virtue: every subject of despotism is equally a slave, but it is difficult for him who spends the greatest part of his time under the ample canopy of heaven, who sees all around him free except himself and his fellow creature man, who feels no immediate benefit from the princes of the earth, and only knows his dependence on them by their temporary oppressions, it is difficult for that being not to consider the great and the rich as his enemies: it is still more difficult for him to disguise that feeling; neither can he conceive the necessity of feigning. It is no mark of illiberal sentiment to neglect those above us: we see and confess the wants of this army, we supply them with what we possess, and should be cruel if we denied them: the connexion which their necessity has made them form with us, engages us to live familiarly

---

[13]*mediocrity*: "Small degree; middle state."

[14]*candour*: "Sweetness of temper; purity of mind; kindness."

together; we communicate to them our ideas, and receive information from them: our obligations are reciprocal, and our desire to please mutual; but where none of these motives subsist, how can you judge of the essential character of any individual, or of any class of people?"

Chapter 9

RASSELAS IN CONFINEMENT

THE ARMY NOW arrived in a spacious plain surrounded by an amphitheatre of hills, where finding excellent pasturage, plentiful springs of water, and a large forest to screen them from the heats of the sun, they formed a regular camp, distributed rewards and punishments, and passed several days in feasts and dissipation. The Arabs, who had accompanied the Egyptians in their unsuccessful expedition, finding that they loitered away much time in a state of inaction, became weary of expectation, and unanimously agreed to leave their allies and return to their ancient desultory mode of fighting; but before they departed, they demanded a division of the spoils and prisoners. The Egyptians being unable to refuse, after they had employed ineffectually all means of soothing them to remain among them, found themselves at last obliged not only to give up their best captives, but to enrich the Arabs with the most precious of their acquisitions; they murmured but they complied. Such is the advantage of the strong and active over the weak and indolent.

Rasselas, in the division of the prisoners, fell to the share of the commander of the Arabs, and was esteemed a valuable prize, on account of his youth, his commanding figure, and his skill in various languages: but it was not convenient for the chief to carry him immediately to Cairo, the great mart for captives, as he would have been embarrassed with him on his march: he therefore placed him with two slaves of approved fidelity, in a strong tower on the summit of an almost inaccessible mountain, and promised to return for him the next month. The slaves by turns descended into the valley to seek provisions for themselves and Rasselas, but, in compliance with what their master had exacted in proof of their fidelity, for some time never exchanged a word with their prisoner.

Rasselas, notwithstanding his former philosophy, daily lost all temper[15] in his present situation: during his journey thither, and after

---

[15]*temper*: "Calmness of mind."

his arrival, he had shewn so great an impatience of control, and so much desire of forcing his guard, that he was kept in uncommon strictness. However disagreeable and humiliating might be the fate which he expected after the return of the Arab, he anxiously counted the days allotted for his confinement: solitude appeared to him the worst of evils, and at the expiration of the month, he looked over the country for the arrival of the Arab with an eager expectation, equal to that with which he would have waited for the return of a friend. From the rising to the setting sun, he passed the day at the window of his prison, and would scarcely leave it to take his accustomed food: for several days following, he remained in the same state of anxiety; his mind seemed absorbed in one idea, and could find no resources in itself. He endeavoured to substitute the thoughts of the past for those of the future: it was impossible – sleep fled from him by night, and repose by day; he interrogated the slaves and received no answer: at last, as they perceived his agitation to be violent, and feared it would endanger his health, they told him their master often came much later than he had designed, since his return depended on the success of his arms; that he might possibly be several months absent, but that in the mean time he himself should experience no other inconveniency than that of confinement.

Chapter 10

THE RESOURCES OF SOLITUDE

THE PRINCE, FAR from being comforted by the answer of the slaves, was overwhelmed with affliction: he sunk hopeless on his mat, the only furniture of his prison, and gave himself up to all the melancholy of his reflections. "I am now," said he, "arrived at the evil I have always dreaded, and which it has been my constant study to avoid – why did I take such pains to quit the happy valley, but to emerge from a state of oblivion and inactivity? Why have I endeavoured all my life to improve in virtue and knowledge, but with the hopes of advancing the good of others and my own glory? To whom now can I communicate my thoughts? From whom can I gain applause or receive information? If the Arab should fall a sacrifice to his avidity, than which nothing is more probable, who will be acquainted with my retreat? Shall I not be condemned to wear out my days in dreadful solitude, without any being to alleviate my woes? The guards, who are placed to watch me, are not only unwilling but incapable of affording me consolation: I have not the resource of conversing with the learned of former ages, since not a volume is to be found within these walls – the power of writing is denied me – I can gain no alleviation of my misery by setting down my thoughts and arranging them with reflection – how poor is man when divested of external succour!"

Nor were these the only reflections of Rasselas: he was anxious for what might be the fate of Nekayah; he recalled to mind, with the most bitter regret, the happy moments he had passed in listening to the eloquence of Imlac, and the science of the astronomer: he often feared that Dinarbas had fallen a victim to his courage, and perhaps to his friendship for him. The image of Zilia was eternally present to him; every situation in which he had found himself with her, every smile, every tear, was fresh in his imagination: he often repeated the conversations he had held with her, and though the remembrance gave him inexpressible pain, he feared the images should decay, and strove to imprint them more strongly on his memory, lest he should lose the only satisfaction that was left him. What gave him the greatest uneasiness, was the fear of being forgotten, and though he felt the improbability that his friends should discover the place of his retreat, his heart would sometimes accuse them of neglect.

In this state of weariness and affliction Rasselas passed near a fortnight; but at length he began insensibly to accustom himself to his situation, and to find amusement from the great objects of nature which alone presented themselves to his view. An awful tempest, exhibiting the most noble contrast of light and darkness, first attracted his attention, and for a few moments made him forget his cares: he therefore pursued this new resource, and watched the various changes of the sky with their effects on the chain of mountains that surrounded him. A clear moonlight, which adorned the hemisphere some evenings after, gave him the first sentiment of pleasure which he had experienced since his captivity: he described his sensations in a small poem which he composed and addressed to Zilia: the pains he took to repeat and retain it in his memory employed the rest of the evening, and he slept that night better than he had done since his imprisonment. The following day he composed a description of the tempest, addressed to Imlac, and resolved, on the first occasion, that the absence of the moon should restore brilliancy to the stars, to dedicate an ode on that subject to the astronomer. At night, as soon as the lunar rays entered his chamber, he flew with rapture to the window, as to a situation that recalled to him more forcibly the image of Zilia; he made some changes in the poem addressed to her the former evening, added some descriptions of the prospect in his view, and retired to rest with more than usual tranquillity.

Nekayah was not forgotten in these ideal[16] compositions, and from the time of his finding this employment, he was less wearied with expectation, and consequently more content with his present situation. He no longer spent hours at the window looking towards the only accessible side of the mountain, nor listened to the noise of the wind, in hopes it might be the trampling of horses. He felt applause in his own mind for this new-acquired patience, as for a victory gained over himself, and the exultation of conscious merit gave new strength to his resolutions.

---

[16]*ideal*: "Mental; intellectual; not perceived by the senses."

Chapter 11

RESIGNATION

RASSELAS WAS NOT only resigned to his fate, but began to be persuaded that his confinement was rather a good than an evil. "How unthinking, and how ungrateful is man!" said he, "how could I prefer the thoughts of slavery and degradation to the life I am now leading! It is true that I am deprived of the amusements of variety, and debarred from the reciprocal communications of friendship, but I am equally saved from the mortifications so frequent in society, and from the malice of hatred and envy. If I am incapacitated from doing good, I am at least prevented from committing ill: it is true I am here useless to my friends, but I have the satisfaction of reflecting that it was in their defence, and in the service of my country that I lost my liberty. – Nekayah has sense and resolution, she can neither want friends to assist her with advice, nor prudence to follow their counsels. Imlac and the astronomer pursued their path in life long before they knew me: Dinarbas either perished nobly in the battle, or is engaged in the career of glory. Zilia – Zilia could never have been mine with honour to herself, and obedience to my father – I am saved from the pain of seeing her in the arms of another, or of destroying all the happiness of her life – Providence has certainly enclosed me here as a shelter from guilt, and I receive the benefit with gratitude.

"The hermit whom we visited in his retreat, and accompanied back to Cairo, was not contented with a voluntary retirement,[17] and yet I have accustomed myself to forced seclusion, even without many of the advantages which he enjoyed – whence arises so strange a difference? Perhaps, while the mind has a power of wandering, it can never sink into repose: perhaps, while choice is allowed us, inconstancy will attend our desires: how merciful is Heaven in allotting to man the part he is to act in this world! Did it depend wholly on himself, caprice would direct his actions, and remorse would follow them.

---

[17]See *Rasselas*, chapter 21.

Resignation should be the favourite study of the wise, and the principal virtue of the brave.

"How can a man think himself alone while surrounded with the noblest works of his Creator? while the planets, the stars, and that great luminary, whose general influence dispenses light and heat to the vast universe, afford a constant field for meditation and thankfulness? How can he consider himself as friendless and unprotected, when the hand of God equally supports the captive in his wretched dungeon, and the conqueror at the head of his triumphant army? when a moment may change the fate of either as his will directs, and when all their efforts, without his immediate assistance, can neither alter or continue their present situation? Uncertain as I am which is the most preferable of the various conditions of life, I am yet persuaded, that if there is much disappointment, there is likewise much comfort to be found in all. I will therefore form no other prayer to the Divinity, than to keep me from crime and error, and teach me to be wholly governed by his will. Would it not be presumption in a blind man to pretend to choose his path? All that he can do is to endeavour, as far as his strength will permit, to walk upright in that which is appointed him by his guide – and are we not all morally blind? What have the greatest sages discovered but that they knew nothing? And shall we not yield ourselves without reserve to the direction of that Divine Leader, who not only allots for us the path it is most fit we should pursue, but supports and consoles us amid the dangers and difficulties that surround it."

Chapter 12

NEKAYAH INSTRUCTED BY MISFORTUNE

DURING THE CONFINEMENT of Rasselas, various events happened in the fortress where he had left Nekayah.

Attended by Imlac, Nekayah went to the apartment of Amalphis: she found him seated on a sofa writing: she was astonished at his tranquillity, and advancing, enquired, with trembling anxiety, after Dinarbas.

"Lady," returned the venerable warrior, "my son is no more – he has fallen nobly in the exercise of his duty; and while the funeral honours, that justly belong to the young hero, are preparing, I take this moment to inform the emperor of the success of his arms." – "Is such then," replied Nekayah, "the effect of philosophy, courage, or resignation? Can they divest you of the feelings of nature, or teach you to support with patience a loss under which the wisest have despaired, and the bravest have sunk?" "Lady," said Amalphis, "neither philosophy nor reason could reconcile me to the death of my son: they who would cure grief by declamation, or stifle sentiment by reason, know little of the heart of man: the more I think, the more I am persuaded of the virtues of Dinarbas: the more I reflect, the more I must regret his loss. My hopes are over in this world, and happiness is for ever banished from me: all that now remains is to do my duty for the poor remnant of my life, and then sink into tranquillity or rise to glory. Grief does not always shew itself by tears and exclamations: if there is any power in philosophy, it consists in preventing us from giving exterior proofs of our affliction, but it cannot cure the wound inflicted on the heart:[18] employment and activity may perhaps have a greater effect, but not in sufferings like mine. The only reflection that saves me on the very brink of the precipice of despair, is resignation to the will of Heaven; and the only motives, that can make me outwardly conquer my affliction, are my duty to my sovereign and

---

[18]Compare *Rasselas*, chapter 18.

my love to Zilia: these," added Amalphis with a look of unutterable sorrow, "make me bear life, nor trouble others with my complaints; but the anguish remains in my breast, and time or reflection will only serve to increase it."

The princess retired abashed, and penetrated with the most poignant grief: she threw herself on her couch, and commanded all her attendants, except Pekuah, to withdraw. "How can I ever forgive myself," said she, "my dear Pekuah, for considering Amalphis as insensible? Is not his the only true philosophy? He is miserable, yet he will support his own character, and do his duty to others – his affliction will prey on his health, and perhaps he will fall a victim to that sentiment of which I supposed him incapable! – and what am I? – how have I treated the hero whom I shall never cease to lament! Pride, where art thou now? – Did I not, from the first moment of my conversing with Dinarbas, find in him all the noble fire of heroism, without vanity or rashness? all the liveliness of wit, and all the depth of knowledge, without ill-nature and without pedantry? Was not my first care to please and interest him, and when I perceived with joy the impression I had made, did I not assume the air of haughty superiority and of mortifying indifference? And why? – because he treated me with peculiar respect – because he wore my chains I made them still more heavy, and used every art to render them lasting: if he had not honoured me with a regard of which I was unworthy, should I not anxiously have sought delight from his eloquence, and instruction from his knowledge! Should I not have been struck with awe and admiration at his virtue! – O power, how dangerous art thou to all! How little to be trusted in the hands of woman! Forgive me, Dinarbas! my whole remaining life, a life of remorse, shall expiate my fault – ."

As Nekayah uttered these words, Zilia entered the apartment: she was dressed in a long mourning robe, her face was veiled, and she was attended by her women, habited in the same manner.

"Nekayah," said she, "I am going to pay the last sad duties to the remains of my brother: the funeral procession advances towards the final habitation of the brave – wilt thou not join me in this melancholy moment? If the dead are conscious of what passes on earth, the spirit of Dinarbas will rejoice in thy respect to his memory; for he loved thee, O Nekayah! and if thy brother was here, he would pay with tears this homage to his friend – he would join me in my grief - ." Nekayah had not power to answer. She made a sign that they should bring her a mourning habit; covered herself with a thick veil, and without pronouncing a word followed the steps of Zilia.

Chapter 13

THE FUNERAL OF DINARBAS

THE BODY OF DINARBAS, clothed in a rich robe, was carried on a bier decorated with branches of palm and laurel, by six of the chosen warriors whom he had commanded, while the rest followed leading their horses, all marching with their arms reversed, to the sound of mournful harmony, with unfeigned affliction in their countenance. Next to them walked Amalphis, followed by Zilia, Nekayah, and their attendants, the procession being closed by the remainder of the garrison. Dinarbas had gained the affection of all, and by all he was regretted.

When they arrived at the place of burial, which was a small valley on the banks of the river, the soldiers set down the bier; and the garrison being formed into ranks, on one side headed by Amalphis, while on the other stood the female mourners, a venerable priest advanced, and according to the custom of Abissinia, placing himself near the body, pronounced the following oration:

"Grieve not, O ye soldiers, companions of the hero whose obsequies we are met to celebrate: your lamentations cannot recal him to life: weep not, ye lovely mourners, Dinarbas cannot be restored by your tears: Attend to the praise of his actions, and imitate his virtues all ye who regret his loss: behold the fate of youth, of genius, of valour! Employ the fleeting hours, and let your life, like his, be glorious, and your death, like his, triumphant.

"Few have been thy years, Dinarbas! but well hast thou employed them: the burning sands of Lybia, the stony precipices of Arabia, the fertile plains of Egypt, have been witnesses of thy glorious deeds: conquest sat on thy sword, and humanity beamed from thy eyes. Unwearied by fatigue and hardship, uncorrupted by the charms of victory, thy mind was active as the northern breeze, and thy heart pure as the stream that flows before thee: fierce as the whirlwind in the day of battle, mild as the zephyr in the hour of friendship, thou knewest all the arts of war, and all the ornaments of peace! merciful to thy vanquished enemies, unshaken in thy resolves, courteous in thy manners, firm and ardent in the cause of honour and of thy country, thou leavest us to lament thy loss, and to follow thy example! – yet who shall imitate thee, O Dinarbas? where shall we find the warmth of youth, united to the experience of age? where shall we see, but in thy comprehensive mind, the knowledge of the sage who has passed his days in meditation, and that of the soldier whose years have flowed through the busy scenes of active life? Warriors! like him fly the seductions of dissipation: Dinarbas, in the bloom of youth, endowed with all the warmth of fancy, was superior to their enticements: his greatest conquests were over his own passions: he subdued them, or like vanquished enemies made them subservient to his great designs, and directed them with despotic sway in the cause of virtue and honour. Superior to every obstacle, when he had by his last action ensured his glory and our freedom, he fell in the arms of victory, and expired amidst the acclamations of a grateful people. – Strew his bier with flowers, O ye virgins of Abissinia! he has saved you from slavery and dishonour – throw palms and laurels around him, O ye warriors! he led you to conquest, and he has left you the fruits of his triumph – and thou, Amalphis! by whom he was inspired with heroic ardour and god-like virtue; thou whose precepts and whose example he has so well obeyed and imitated, father of our hero, and father of thy troops! may the great exploits, may the exalted virtues of Dinarbas compensate to thee the shortness of the term which Heaven has granted him! and may these, thy other children, emulate equally the valour and the filial affection of their beloved warrior!"

Amalphis could no longer refrain from tears; they trickled in abundance down his venerable cheeks; the chiefs of the army ran to embrace his knees, and the soldiers, whom respect detained from approaching, filled the air with exclamations of grief for Dinarbas, and vows of fidelity to his father.

Zilia and Nekayah remained motionless in silent sorrow: the priest made signs for them to advance and cast flowers on the bier: they approached with trembling knees, and uncertain steps: the tender Zilia supported herself, half fainting, on her women; but Nekayah, summoning all her resolution to pay the last tribute to the memory of Dinarbas, walked majestically to the bier, and looking steadfastly on the body, as she scattered roses over it, thought she perceived the breast heave with some remains of life: dubious and agitated between hope and fear, she approached still nearer, when she saw his eyes open, and again close from the light of day, and soon after a sigh assured her he was yet alive. "No longer mourn, but assist your hero," cried Nekayah, wild with joy, and yet trembling with apprehension; "bring speedy succour, and he may still be preserved to his friends and country – he yet breathes – O haste to save him!"

The rapture and confusion were universal. Amalphis thought that the imagination of Nekayah, affrighted at the mournful solemnity, had flattered her disturbed senses with a momentary delusion: the most skilful physicians, the whole garrison, had pronounced him dead. Amalphis raised his eyes to Heaven – "Defend me, all-gracious Power!" cried the venerable warrior, "defend me from this dazzling ray of fallacious hope, save me from falling still deeper into the abyss of misery."

Chapter 14

EMBARRASSMENT OF NEKAYAH

BY THE CARE OF THOSE around him, Dinarbas was restored to life: he turned his eyes with astonishment on Nekayah, Zilia, and his father. Amalphis could no longer doubt: he poured forth his grateful thanks to Heaven with all the feelings of a father, and ordered his son to be carried back to his apartment in the fortress, where, in a few days, his wounds were proved not to be mortal.

Nekayah was in the mean time greatly embarrassed with her own reflections: she was sensible that as soon as Dinarbas was recovered he would renew his visits to her: the supposed obligation of her restoring him to life would be a strong claim upon his gratitude, and he could therefore no longer avoid her company even if he wished it: his distant respect must change into tender acknowledgements, and she could not trust her heart with receiving them. She now wanted counsel, and knew not where to seek it: Rasselas, in whom she had the highest confidence, was absent: Pekuah was too submissively attached to her mistress to have any other opinion than hers: Imlac she suspected of the same complaisance,[19] and the astronomer was too unknowing in the ways of the world to afford her any assistance. Amalphis and Zilia were the last persons to whom she could have applied, even if they had been acquainted with her situation, which she did not choose to disclose to them. In this perplexity of doubt, her mind often rested on the idea of Dinarbas. "Did not my sentiments too nearly regard himself," thought Nekayah, "how excellent a friend might I have found in him! one in whom my confidence would have been securely placed, and whose judgment and sincerity would have directed me in the paths of honour and of prudence!"

Such were the anxieties of Nekayah, and she soon had reason to perceive they were not groundless.

---

[19]*complaisance*: "Civility; desire of pleasing; act of adulation."

Dinarbas recovered his health, and his first care was to visit her. Zilia had informed him of the grief which the princess had felt for his loss, and the respect she had paid to his memory. His father had related to him the circumstances of his being restored to life by Nekayah, and the joy that had appeared in her countenance. She had indeed foreseen that all this would happen; but she could not have solicited a concealment of her sentiments without giving a suspicion of their nature.

When she perceived Dinarbas enter the apartment, she endeavoured to hide her agitation, and turned the discourse on the universal joy of the garrison at his recovery, and particularly on the feelings of his father and Zilia: she smilingly mentioned the praises which had been bestowed on him at his funeral, and congratulated the young warrior on the rare advantage of being informed of them: she then changed the subject, talked of her brother, and of the fruitless enquiries made by Amalphis after the Egyptian army. But Dinarbas was not satisfied with the apparent ease with which she spoke of circumstances that, by the account of Zilia, had so deeply affected her.

"Nekayah," said he, "do not expect me to thank you for restoring me to life; my death would have been happy: I had done my duty, and my father and fellow soldiers approved my actions: my sister had shown her regard for my memory; and I am told, that even Nekayah shed some tears over me – Had I been sensible of so unexpected and so blest an event, I could have desired no more. I am now restored to life and to your indifference; yet, Nekayah, you are mistaken in Dinarbas, if you suppose him capable of passing the bounds of that respect which he owes you: his conduct might have assured you of his efforts to subdue a passion, of which he is no longer master, and for which you ought rather to pity than to blame him."

"Dinarbas!" answered the princess, "I will be sincere with you; I own my fault in not having sooner been so: hear me, and learn the reasons of my conduct; but first let me entreat your promise never, till you see my brother, to disclose the secret with which I am going to entrust you."

Dinarbas promised all she desired, and Nekayah continued, "I am daughter to the emperor of Abissinia, and Rasselas is his fourth son:

curiosity after new scenes, and disgust of[20] inaction, first induced us to leave the valley; you know the rest; – judge whether I ought to hear you; judge, when I further confess, that I hear you with pleasure."

Dinarbas was less surprised at the discovery of the rank of Nekayah, than delighted with her avowal of an attachment, which he could scarcely have hoped for; he was about to thank her with all the raptures of happy love, when the princess stopped him.

"Dinarbas," said she, "the discovery I have made to you is not to authorise your weakness or mine: the confidence I have placed in you, proves my opinion of your prudence, and my conviction of your honour. Pleased with the charms of your society, secure in your respect, and conscious of my own principles, I should perhaps have remained a long time in the delightful illusion, without thinking of the uneasiness I was preparing for myself and for you: but, I had no right to leave you in error, and your conduct has deserved that I should explain myself: after this explanation, I fly to you for counsel and support: assist me in clearing the mist which obscures our reason. It is true I consider as a prejudice the difference of our birth; but it is a prejudice established by the universal custom of ages, and consequently ought to be respected by all who regard their fame: virtue is wholly in our power, but fame depends on the breath of the multitude, and the multitude is governed by prejudice."

---

[20]*disgust of*: aversion to.

Chapter 15

DINARBAS JUSTIFIES THE CONFIDENCE OF THE PRINCESS

DINARBAS, ASTONISHED and distressed at the discourse of Nekayah, remained for some time silent; at length recovering himself, "Princess," said he, "I will not ask your pardon for involuntary error: I thank you for the confidence you have reposed in me: you will soon judge whether I deserve it: only remember that though we may be masters of our actions, we cannot command our sentiments: mine will never alter; but your sincerity has found the only means of imposing on them an eternal silence."

Having so said, he left abruptly the apartment. Nekayah arose, went to the window, and raising her eyes to heaven, "All-seeing Power!" said she, "support me in this hour of trial, this hour in which Nekayah has resigned all the happiness of her life: I feel the whole weight of the sacrifice; I find I was not deceived in Dinarbas."

A short time after, Amalphis entered: "Lady," said he, "my son is resolved to seek his friend: the captivity of your brother will not permit him to continue longer in a repose which he thinks degrading to his honour, and injurious to his friendship. I approve his intention, but not the desire of its immediate execution: his wounds are recent, his health not yet re-established; join your entreaties to mine, and he will perhaps delay for a few days his departure: my counsels, nay my commands have been fruitless." Zilia, who at this instant entered the apartment, made the same request to Nekayah with tears in her eyes. The princess was more embarrassed than ever, yet could find no reason to refuse so just a prayer: she sent for Dinarbas, and, before his father and Zilia, thanked him for his generous resolution; but requested that he would defer to put it in execution till his health should be perfectly restored.

From this moment, she studiously avoided all occasions of meeting Dinarbas, except in company with Pekuah, Imlac, and the astronomer, whose lively and instructive conversation always found new subjects, and prevented the fatal vacuity which Nekayah dreaded; yet could not all her endeavours stop the increasing ill: the constraint, which both the princess and Dinarbas imposed on themselves, served only to augment their mutual esteem, and consequently defeated their intentions.

Imlac, without penetrating the cause of an uneasiness which he had long perceived in the princess, imagined the activity of her mind wanted new objects; and that fatigued with always seeing the same things, and pursuing the same topics, she was weary of her situation, and of all that surrounded her. He therefore endeavoured to find out some novelty that might fix her attention; and having been himself greatly delighted with the conversation of the priest who had pronounced the funeral oration of Dinarbas, he entreated leave of the princess to introduce him to her. Nekayah gladly accepted the proposal: his discourse on that memorable day was deeply engraved on her mind, and she had often wished for an opportunity of conversing with him.

Elphenor was surprised at the proposal of Imlac. "Immersed as I have been for more than forty years," said he, "in the studies necessary to my profession, what entertainment can my conversation afford to youth and beauty, gaiety and wit? Your lady will behold in me a man, who has given up all connexions in this world, except with those individuals whose miseries lead them to apply to me for assistance. I have been long disused to the society of the fortunate: however, I will neither refuse the solicitations of kindness, nor the request of curiosity: I will accompany you whenever you command me."

Chapter 16

ADVANTAGES AND DISADVANTAGES OF THE SACERDOTAL STATION

THE PRINCESS, PEKUAH and the astronomer, were waiting with impatience for the arrival of Imlac with the priest: at their entrance, the princess rose and respectfully saluted Elphenor: he returned her courtesy with a modest, but not servile humility; and the conversation soon became general: it turned on the happy event which had restored Dinarbas to his friends; and the princess took occasion to bestow the warmest praises on the oration pronounced by Elphenor. "Lady," answered he, "whatever impression my words may have made on the assembly, you are not to attribute it to the powers of eloquence. I will not, by a false delicacy,[21] deny that I have been sometimes flattered with exciting the applauses of my auditors, and that I have passed days and nights in studying to deserve them; but my late theme was of itself sufficient to interest those who heard me, and the hearts of all the assembly felt more than the most studied discourse could inspire. If they approved of my words, it was because they perceived my feelings were congenial with their own: in courts and in great cities, the flowers of eloquence may be employed, with successful seduction, to persuade the multitude into an admiration of the imaginary virtues and the nugatory exploits of those whom we are commanded to celebrate: the veil of dignity which conceals them from the people, the uncertainty of opinions which disguises them amongst their equals, favour the deception, and hide the falsity of the orator. But in a place like this, where every one had been witness of the life, and could almost dive into the heart of him whom I undertook to propose as a model for their imitation, ornament would have been vain, and deceit useless: besides, I have long since given up the honours of elocution; and all my present aim is, as far as mortal frailty will admit, to pay due homage to truth, and to seize every opportunity of conveying instruction and consolation to those

---

[21]*delicacy*: a refined feeling of what is becoming, modest, or proper (OED).

committed to my care."

"This is the noblest of all aims," replied the princess, "and the only one really worthy of the good and the enlightened: your occupations, venerable Elphenor! are so far above the common pursuits of mankind, that we cannot but consider you in a state infinitely superior to the rest of the inhabitants of this globe. What other profession consecrates itself wholly to the service of the Divinity, and to the comfort of our fellow creatures?"

"My profession," answered the sage, "is certainly deserving of reverence and protection; but where is the state of life in which a man cannot meditate on the power and goodness of the Deity? in which he cannot assist and instruct other human beings? It is true, we are peculiarly set apart for these duties; but do we always perform them? If we do not, how far more guilty are we than the rest of mortals, who have other employments, other avocations to divert their attention? Sensible of the awful charge committed to our care, how poignant must be our remorse, if we have omitted the means of guiding our disciples, if we have led them astray by false maxims or bad example – !"

Here Elphenor made a short pause, but soon added, with unusual warmth, – "And where is the instructor who has nothing of this kind with which to reproach himself? Yet let me add, whatever may be the faults, whatever the negligence of the members of our order, we are often too severely punished by the strictures of the world: the smallest error in our conduct, the smallest weakness in our nature is harshly condemned, or cruelly ridiculed by the multitude, whose eyes, ever open to the failings of their fellow creatures, are particularly intent on ours. We often deserve blame, I confess, and mankind has the same right to censure us, as the other inhabitants of the globe; but at least let their censure be equally distributed, and let not a larger share than we deserve fall on our heads. Let them consider, that however our thoughts are raised to heaven, our origin is the same as theirs; that we have the same inclinations, the same passions as themselves; and whether the habits and restraints of the clerical life give us greater means of resisting them or not, is to me uncertain: either therefore the whole world is unjust, or our profession has no advantages superior to those of other men."

"You have at least," said Imlac, "the advantage of being and having been in every age, and in every nation, the class of men to whom every one has applied for counsel, and whom the greater number have obeyed without hesitation. You enjoy the most flattering of all distinctions, that of respect; and you exercise the most powerful of all jurisdictions, for your empire is exercised over the mind: your influence has been equally felt in the great revolutions of kingdoms, and in the management of domestic concerns. While you enjoy these distinguished prerogatives, can you wonder that envy should attack you, or that mankind, naturally impatient of subjection, should take the first opportunity of emancipating itself from that respect, to which it submits with pain, because enjoined as a duty."

"These very prerogatives," answered Elphenor, "are the greatest enemies that we have to fear: dazzled with the specious titles lavished on us by the world, convinced of the real advantages to be reaped from power and influence, pride has taken possession of so many individuals among us, that censure has often called it the distinctive character of our order; and as simplicity and truth have only power to govern rational minds, many of us who have aimed at universal dominion, have thought it necessary to employ other means to catch the greater number. We have had recourse to the assistance of pomp and luxury to command the respect of the vain, and have armed ourselves with all the terrors of superstition to subdue the ignorant, the fearful, and the weak. Such have been the errors into which ambition has led us, errors more hurtful to mankind, than all the destruction which has followed the sword of the General, or the projects of the Statesman."

Chapter 17

DANGER OF FANATICISM

NEKAYAH, DELIGHTED with the candour of Elphenor, told him that she was assured he had no reason to reproach himself with the ills mankind had suffered by men of his order; and that she doubted not but many others, though they might not have attained to the height of beneficence and exemplary conduct which distinguished him, yet had, to the best of their knowledge, fulfilled the duty of their station.

"Indeed, Lady," answered the sage, "I have known many to whom I have looked up with reverence, many who have subdued their passions with heroism, and who have devoted themselves entirely to their functions; I have seen amongst my brethren some examples of uncommon fortitude, some who in times of that most dreadful scourge of human nature, general pestilence, have steadfastly remained with their disciples to encourage and console them, when universal terror had broken even the ties of blood, and when the fear of death alone reigned with despotic sway. I have known others who, firm in the cause of religion, have sacrificed their life to their belief: but here much distinction is to be made: obstinately attached to his opinion, a man often mistakes hypothesis for truth: and will often go as far in its defence. Every religion has had its martyrs, whose deaths frequently inspire us with less admiration of their constancy, than abhorrence of the cruelty of their intolerant persecutors."

"Sir," said the astronomer, "your discourse convinces me not only of your sincerity, but of your judgment: I am therefore persuaded you will forgive me, if I ask you whether your piety is not often shocked, and your understanding disgusted, at finding yourself obliged by the laws of Abissinia, not only to practice, but to enjoin to others, some ceremonies which you cannot approve. Are you not grieved to find, that many of the more enlightened part of your disciples doubt of the most essential truths of our religion, on account of the accessory circumstances invented by man? and to see that the lower class of those committed to your care, embrace equally the practices of exalted piety and of senseless fanaticism, while with affecting, though mistaken zeal, they follow blindly every error into which custom compels you to lead them?"²²

"That I have felt all the sentiments you now describe," replied Elphenor, "you will scarcely believe, when you see me pursue the practices which you so justly disapprove; yet nothing is more true. I venerate the unsullied purity of religion, and lament that it should be encompassed with the veil of superstition; but some ceremonies are necessary, and they who have endeavoured to divest it totally of such, have found that reverence has been laid aside, and respect forgotten, while fanaticism has taken the same hold of the ignorant, though it has assumed a different form. Error is natural to man: the wayward mind will ever substitute superstition for devotion, and sophistry for philosophy. Where can you see this more exemplified than in the science which you have made your particular study? During how many ages has not the strangest of all errors, judicial astrology, prevailed over the senses of man, while the demonstrations of astronomical truth have been neglected? With respect to those, whom you call the more enlightened part of my hearers, who condemn the whole of religion because some accessory circumstances are faulty, they have likewise their incomprehensible tenets and their particular fanaticism; and it has been justly remarked, that none is more credulous than the unbeliever."

"Alas!" rejoined Nekayah, "who would madly give up the only consolation in the time of affliction, the only refuge for grief, the only calmer of inquietude? Without the aiding power of religion, we should be abandoned to despair – what other means could we find to conquer those sentiments and subdue those afflictions which give way only to the prevalence of devotion."

"It is certain," answered the sage, "religion is the universal and the only true consoler; yet I must add, that from this maxim, true as it is, often springs a most fatal error: the mind, weakened by affliction, falls more easily a victim to the baneful influence of fanaticism; and when once it has begun to wander in the gloomy mansions of that destructive phantom, its energy is wholly lost, and it is conducted by its haughty ruler amid the mazes of deception, till it loses not only the

---

²²Knight regarded many elements of Catholicism as "a mockery of religion" (Kaye, 2:218).

hope, but even the desire of returning happiness.

"My situation has often afforded me examples of this truth; and I have been so much convinced of the danger, that, whenever the afflicted apply to me, after I have exhorted them to hope in the beneficence of that Being, who can raise the humble from the dust, calm every discordant passion, and restore peace and tranquillity to the bosom lacerated by disappointed ambition or hopeless love, I always counsel them to avoid meditation, to fly from solitude, as the most pernicious of evils, and seek in employment a refuge from morbid care.

"The greatest of all mental afflictions, the consciousness of guilt, may be lessened by deprecating[23] the wrath of offended Heaven, and by the exercise of active virtue; but to substitute indolent fanaticism for criminal pursuits, is only exchanging one passion for another, and losing those precious moments which a merciful Deity has granted for expiatory repentance."

---

[23]*deprecating*: imploring mercy of.

Chapter 18

TROUBLES IN ABISSINIA

NEKAYAH WAS STRUCK with the advice of Elphenor, and felt the necessity of exercising the virtues he recommended.

The time now approached which had been fixed for the departure of Dinarbas, and every motive engaged him to hasten it: he selected only a few horsemen to accompany him, that he might not leave the fortress unprovided in case of a second attack, and, to the regret of the whole garrison, set forward on an expedition of which the success was uncertain.

The first days of his absence were spent by the princess in reflections on her conduct; and these reflections being naturally consolatory, she applauded her firmness, and hoped that returning tranquillity would soon be the reward of the sacrifice which she had made: but after some time passed in these thoughts, which were only interrupted by the usual occurrences of society, she felt every hour increasing weariness. Unwilling to suppose her victory incomplete, she attributed her anxiety and restlessness to the uncertainty of her fate, to the situation of her brother, to a thousand causes, none of which had occurred to her a few days before. One morning, as she was immersed in these contemplations, Pekuah entered, and informed her that the messenger, dispatched to the court of Abissinia, was returned, and desired admittance. The princess was alarmed at this intelligence: for how could she quit the fortress and return to the happy valley, without her brother?

The messenger, after he had prostrated himself before Nekayah, delivered to her letters directed to the prince, which she received and placed beside her on the sofa: he then, by her command, related, that being arrived at Gonthar, the capital of Abissinia, he had found an universal confusion spread over the city.[24] "The second and third

---

[24]Gondar, a village in the province of Amhara, became the capital of Abyssinia (modern Ethiopia) in the 17th century; handsome palaces, castles, and churches were

sons," said he, "of your glorious father, Sarza and Menas, have rebelled against him, and the venerable monarch is almost a prisoner in his court: these princes, with whose ambitious characters you are not unacquainted, found means to escape from the happy valley by the same passage which prince Rasselas had made: they have raised a considerable army, and are already masters of the fertile province of Amhara. The emperor, on hearing of their revolt, took arms with celerity and marched against them, having first obliged his eldest son Zengis to accompany him and head the cavalry; but this unfortunate prince being lately killed in a skirmish with some of the insurgents, grief and despair have taken possession of the heart of the emperor, who has returned to his capital surrounded by his best troops, leaving the rest under the command of his generals in the field.

"When he received the letter of prince Rasselas, he burst into tears and said – 'I pardon him for leaving the happy valley, though, had he not divested himself of his obedience to his sovereign and father, Sarza and Menas would never have dared to attempt an escape superior to their courage and to their penetration. Go to Rasselas, command him to come to me immediately and expiate his fault by the defence of his father: let Nekayah remain where she now is; but recommend to them both a total silence on their rank, as necessary in the present circumstances, lest Rasselas should be intercepted by his rebellious brothers. My further instructions to him, and the order for the governor of the fortress to set him at liberty, shall be delivered to thee before thy departure.' These are the papers, lady! and the commands of our sovereign: I am not surprised at the astonishment which I perceive in your looks: the rebellion of the princes has been sudden, and is conducted with such art as to prevent all communication between the capital and the frontiers: I had the utmost difficulty to escape their guards; but I will not trouble you with a recital of the various disguises I have employed to elude their vigilance."

---

built, but assassinations, usurpations, and civil wars caused the city to decline after the mid 18th century.

Chapter 19

THE SAME SUBJECT CONTINUED

THE PRINCESS FELT deeply the affliction of her father, and the misfortunes of the state: she reflected seriously on the share she had in causing them, and lamented her total inability of being useful to the emperor: she found herself destitute of all assistance: Rasselas was absent, and in a situation that made it impossible to estimate the time of his return: Dinarbas was, in compliance with her wishes, departed in search of him; and she was deprived of the present aid of that young warrior, without knowing whether he might succeed in finding the prince: she was equally perplexed to know what directions ought to be given to Amalphis in the present emergency. Pekuah conjured her to open the packet addressed to Rasselas; but she firmly refused. "My dear Pekuah," said the princess, "an action which in itself is blameable can never be justified by the lawfulness of the motive: to open a letter addressed to another, is a breach of confidence, which political reasons may authorize, but which honour and delicacy must ever reject. I know not what orders the emperor may have given to Rasselas: I know his commands to me, and will obey them."

The princess then ordered the messenger to repair to Amalphis, and inform him of the rebellion, and of every thing that he was permitted to tell; of her intention of remaining with Zilia, to be in safety from the horrors of war, and of the commands imposed on Rasselas by his sovereign, to fly to his assistance.

Amalphis soon received from various persons the same intelligence of the flame which had made such rapid progress in Abissinia. Precautions may be observed, and respected for a short time by a numerous army; but that will not remain a secret which many are enjoined to keep, and many interested to divulge. Not having received any instructions from the emperor, he was uncertain how to act; for despotic power will not even be served against its commands: he was likewise informed, that a strong body of the enemy's troops had cut off all communication with the capital: the fortress which he commanded, could not make a sufficient defence against the army of the princes, if they advanced to attack it; and the Egyptians might invest it during his absence, if he attempted to march to the assistance of the emperor. Duty and prudence both determined him not to abandon his post, but to wait the event with patience.

Every day, however, increased the anxiety of Amalphis, and redoubled the agitation of Nekayah. New reports of the success of the princes, and of the want of conduct of the royal army, succeeded each other; but in the midst of their inquietudes, they had the satisfaction of receiving an embassy sent by the new Bassa of Cairo, to make excuses to the governor for the hostilities committed by the Egyptians under the influence of his predecessor. The sultan had no sooner been informed of this unauthorized war, than he punished the ambitious Bassa, and appointed another, who was directed to make reparation for the injuries, to restore the prisoners, and chastise the delinquents. The envoy informed Amalphis, that a large body of Turkish horse had been sent to enforce the orders of the sultan against the Egyptians and Arabs, who had so rashly enlisted themselves under the standard of the late Bassa. Amalphis informed him what prisoners had been made in his district, and particularly mentioned Rasselas as having been taken in the sally.

The envoy promised that the most diligent enquiries should be made; and Amalphis, Nekayah, and Zilia conceived the warmest hopes of the approaching liberty of Rasselas.

Chapter 20

THE PRINCE GIVES PROOF OF REAL COURAGE

RASSELAS HAD BEEN now several months in confinement, and, from comparing in his mind the various conditions of life, and calculating the resources of resignation and philosophy, he had reasoned himself into a state of tranquillity nearly resembling content. The slaves who served him had again relapsed into the obstinate silence which they had been enjoined by their master; but Rasselas at length perceived an uneasiness, and even a terror in their looks, of which he in vain enquired the cause.

One day he was surprised to find that at the usual hour of repast no nourishment was brought him, and felt great uneasiness when night drew near and no one appeared: he listened, but could not hear the accustomed sound of the voices of the slaves: no light was reflected on the ground from the narrow window of their chamber, which was under his own: he called to them, but received no answer: at length he thought he heard the noise of footsteps: he repeated his call, when the slave, whose companion had not returned that day with the usual provisions from the valley, and who was gone out to seek him, again entered the tower, but being alone would not enter the chamber of Rasselas, lest his prisoner should attempt the recovery of his liberty. The prince passed the night without sleep, and at break of day perceived the slave departing from the tower: in vain did he call to him, the slave only hastened his pace towards the valley. Rasselas composed himself with the idea that he was probably gone to seek provisions, and that the negligence of the other slave, in not returning the day before, had been the cause of his remaining that day without food; but this day, like the former, being spent in vain expectation, the solicitude of the prince was now changed into apprehension of the most horrid of deaths. All was silent and desolate around him; darkness came on without the consoling prospect of rest, and the last dreadful hour of fate seemed to draw near without the hopes of relief or the balm of pity.

Rasselas had faced death with intrepidity in the rage of battle, but its present silent and cold approaches were far different: a greater share of courage was here necessary to subdue, unaided by the voice of glory, the horrors of dissolution, and a more exalted resignation must inspire him, to abandon every tie that can endear existence, without giving the last counsels, and without taking the last farewell.

Yet had the prince fortitude sufficient to resign himself to the will of Heaven, and to await, without impatience, the close of this scene of solitary wo.

Sleep, which flies from agitation, may yet naturally follow resignation. Rasselas had passed some time in the calm of oblivion, when an unusual noise awakened him, and he had scarcely time to rise before he saw his chamber door burst open, and several armed Turks enter his apartment: their chief informed him that they were sent for his deliverance, and had orders to conduct him to the fortress commanded by Amalphis.

He told him the resentment of the sultan, and the injunctions he had laid on his troops to make diligent search after the prisoners, and informed him they had discovered his retreat by intercepting the slaves: the first, he said, would not betray his trust, but the second, more fearful or more compassionate, had guided them to the path by which alone the tower was accessible.

Chapter 21

THE PRINCE RETURNS TO THE FORTRESS

IDEAS LONG BANISHED from the mind of Rasselas, or considered by him merely as illusions, now returned with new-acquired force: he seemed to endeavour to retrieve in a moment all the time he had lost in solitude; he crowded question on question, but soon had his attention wholly engrossed by the intelligence which the Turks gave him of the rebellion of his brothers.

Grief and remorse took possession of all his faculties, and, without knowing the manner of the escape of the princes, or thinking on the reproaches of his father, he already condemned himself for having, though from innocent motives, set them the example of disobedience: he was now more than ever convinced of the evils arising from a capricious love of change, and of the necessity that every man should be content with the station in which he is placed. "To my own restless disposition," said Rasselas to himself, "I owe the humiliation of fruitless enquiry, the disgrace and weariness of imprisonment, the pangs of hopeless love, and the remorse of not only having destroyed the peace of my father and of my country, but of having driven my brothers into the most odious crimes."

The prince, in consequence of these reflections, entreated the Turks to hasten their march, till with astonishing rapidity they arrived at the fortress commanded by Amalphis: here Rasselas heard a distinct account of the rebellion of his brothers, and received the letter of the emperor from the princess, who anxiously enquired of Rasselas whether he owed his liberty to Dinarbas, relating to him the exertions of friendship in that young warrior. The prince felt all the warmth of gratitude and affection, and bitterly regretted the absence of his generous friend: he then hastily read over the letters that explained to him the present state of his sovereign, who, after having tenderly reproached him for abandoning the happy valley, conjured him to come to his assistance, take command of the army, and assume the regal power. "I am too old," says the emperor, "to direct the thunderbolts of war, or to hold the balance of justice: come and receive the imperial diadem from the hand of thy father: conquer and punish thy rebellious brothers, whom blind affection might lead me to spare: let Nekayah remain with the brave Amalphis, whose virtues and services have been long known to me, and whom long since I should have promoted to higher employments, had I not considered his usefulness on the frontiers: his fidelity is approved, yet make him not acquainted with thy rank, or that of thy sister: I do not think he would betray you to Sarza; but it would not be prudent to give him so great a claim to reward, as the known protection of a son and daughter of the emperor of Abissinia."

This letter made a singular impression on Rasselas: he venerated his father, and was averse to commit a second time the fault of disobedience: yet his humanity was shocked at the idea of depriving his brothers of their right of succession; and he recoiled with horror from the thoughts of their punishment. His generosity was equally disgusted at the diffidence[25] and unthankfulness shewn by the emperor towards a man, whose fidelity he confessed, and whose bravery he admired. The prince then perused the imperial mandate, which he was to deliver to Amalphis, wherein the governor was informed that Rasselas and Nekayah were the children of one of the emperor's favourite emirs; that Rasselas was to have permission to repair immediately to court, and that Nekayah was to remain under the protection of the governor.

The prince, having debated an instant in his own mind, now thought himself at liberty to consult his inclinations: all his filial deference for a father could not induce him to imitate his ingratitude; he sought the good old warrior, delivered to him the emperor's mandate, and spoke thus.

"I must depart, Amalphis, and have not words to express my sense of the important services which you have done me: to you I owe, not only protection and support, but instruction and kindness: without you I should have nothing at present to offer to the emperor but rash and unskilful valour, or at best but idle theory without practice. You have taught me the only true philosophy, resignation and patience: I leave you overwhelmed with obligations, yet I must entreat you to add one more, and that the greatest which you have in your power to

---

[25]*diffidence*: "Distrust."

confer: promise to make me happy in the possession of Zilia; let me be assured by your unerring faith, that you will consent she shall be my wife, when the troubles of Abissinia are appeased, and I shall depart contented."

Amalphis read the emperor's mandate, respectfully kissed the signature, and said, "My sovereign's orders shall be obeyed – as for your request, Sir, I thank you for the honour you are disposed to confer on my family; but, contrary to the custom of our country, I disclaim all right over the choice of Zilia: if she consents, I shall be happy to bestow her on a man, whose conduct and principles I have ever esteemed, and whose kindness I am ambitious to preserve: permit me to consult her inclinations; Zilia is sincere, and will soon determine my answer."

Chapter 22

THE POWER OF ARTIFICE

ZILIA WAS NEITHER unacquainted with the sentiments of Rasselas, nor insensible to them: she had indeed endeavoured to suppress her sensibility, because she could see no reason for the concealment of his rank from her, and none to prevent his demanding her of Amalphis, whom she informed of all that had past in her mind on this occasion, freely submitting to him what answer should be given to Rasselas.

Amalphis smiled, and, introducing Rasselas, acceded to every hope of their mutual affection, with tears of paternal benediction.

Nekayah took her brother aside, and imparted to him all her conversations with Dinarbas: he forbore to make remarks on her story; for happiness cannot easily console, and has no right to upbraid disappointment.

After a few moments given to kindness and gratitude, Rasselas quitted the fortress, and, conducted by the messenger, whose precautions for avoiding a discovery were again successful, arrived at Gonthar, the capital of the kingdom of Abissinia. He found the city in a general consternation, though the forces of the princes were still at a considerable distance. The emperor, surrounded by a few aged counsellors, who had never distinguished themselves in their youth, and whose timidity and indolence had increased with their years, was divided between fear and anger: the punishment of the rebel princes was alone the theme of debate, while every measure was taken to guard against their approach.

In the mean time, desertions were frequent in the royal army, the chiefs of which were tyrannical without firmness, and profuse without liberality: their pomp and magnificence demanded continual supplies, and exhausted the province in which they were encamped: they did not choose to hazard either their reputation or their safety in a general engagement, and they were usually defeated in the skirmishes with which they were perpetually harrassed by the princes. Had these continued to conduct themselves with discernment, and profited by the advantages daily given them, they would have made the most rapid progress; but division had taken possession of their camp. Sarza was of a haughty and violent temper; sudden in his resolves, and uncertain in their execution; prodigal even to madness, and openly avowing the most reprehensible inclinations, which he spared no means to gratify; impatiently desirous of attaining his end, yet neglecting in the arms of pleasure, the steps necessary for obtaining success.

Menas, with no less ambition, had a more regular plan and more apparent modesty: his vices were more cautiously concealed from the eye of public stricture, and his love of pleasure was flattered by the hopes of a crown, which would put him in possession of all he could desire: he acted apparently for his brother, and industriously gave out that he had no other wish than to place the diadem on the head of Sarza; yet he laboured to form a party, that might support him in his pretensions, when his brother by his imprudence should have lost the affections of the people; which he thought must inevitably happen, on his ascending the throne of Abissinia. Though at present the minds of the multitude were much more favourable to the splendid Sarza than to the cautious Menas, as the exterior accomplishments of the former were more striking, his temerity being denominated heroism, and his love of pleasure popularity, yet the steps of Menas towards power, were more sure; and as he had been the instigator of the attempt, so he was the supporter of it; though all the nation considered Sarza as the only author of the enterprize.

Such were the enemies whom Rasselas was commanded by his father to oppose, and these enemies his own brothers!

As soon as he arrived at the camp, he was invested by the generals with the supreme command: his first care was to introduce discipline and frugality among the troops: he succeeded in his attempt without losing their affection; and set them that example which virtue or shame obliged them to follow. When he thought his army sufficiently disciplined to face that of the enemy, he advanced towards the kingdom of Amhara, and met the rebels on a large plain near the city of Bagemder; where he ordered his troops to halt, and having formed them into order of battle, sent a messenger to demand a conference with his brothers.

Chapter 23

RASSELAS ENDEAVOURS TO PRODUCE A RECONCILIATION

THE TWO PRINCES advanced to meet Rasselas into the middle of the plain, and, after a royal pavilion had been erected, entreated him to enter; but Rasselas declined the offer, and insisted on their conference being held in the open air, and in sight of the two armies.

He began by an enquiry into the cause of their impious rebellion, and received for an answer, the usual pretences for insurrection, complaints of the emperor, artfully veiled in respectful terms, open accusations of his favourites and ministers, zeal for the public good, and dread of increasing evils.

Rasselas replied, that they were sons and subjects of the emperor, and that, whatever might be the faults of government, they were not authorized, either by the nation, or by its chief, to attempt a reformation: he entered deeply into considerations of the respect due to the monarch and the father; of the baneful influence of the spirit of mutiny; and of the danger of foreign invasion, while the arms of Abissinia were turned against herself. He finished by conjuring the princes to return to their duty, and by accusing himself of having, by his departure from the happy valley, given them the first example of disobedience: he promised them unconditional pardon, and a general amnesty to their troops.

Sarza was affected at the discourse of Rasselas, which was sometimes pathetic and sometimes forcible, and seemed willing to enter into a treaty of accommodation, of which he deferred the execution till the next day, by the advice of Menas.

The different sentiments of the brothers had not escaped the observation of Rasselas: he knew the character of each, and felt all that was to be apprehended from the dangerous influence of Menas. He retired into his tent, hopeless of reconciliation, the expectation of which was general in the two armies; but Rasselas knew that Sarza was only to be prevailed on by sudden starts of conviction, and that, if he delayed to follow the momentary ray of virtue, he became the victim of the first seducer whose interest it was to present a different counsel in a plausible light: he wanted that firmness, without which virtue is useless, and understanding merely an illusion.

These reflections distressed the prince: whenever he turned his thoughts on the continuation of the war, he saw nothing but horror, whether in conquest or defeat: sometimes however he would think that he had conceived too harsh an opinion of the character of Menas, and sometimes he flattered himself that Sarza would have sufficient energy to withstand his insinuations.

As he was seated in his tent, waiting with impatience for the morning, a stranger was announced whom he perceived, through the disguise that covered him, to be his brother Menas: he commanded his attendants to withdraw, and then enquired the occasion of his visit.

"Thou mayest see, Rasselas," said Menas, "the confidence I place in thy generosity: I come to treat with thee, and to free myself from every suspicion that may have arisen in thy breast against me: thou knowest the headstrong disposition of Sarza: ambition and ill counsellors enflamed him with a desire of seizing the reins of government, and enclosing his father in the palace of the valley, there to finish his days in peaceful pleasures. After vainly endeavouring to dissuade him from an enterprize, which, whatever might be its motive, must always have the appearance of disobedience, I offered to accompany him, flattering myself that I should be able to set some bounds to the impetuosity of his temper, and save both my father and the nation from the tempest which menaced them. Hitherto I have so far succeeded, as to prevent unnecessary effusion of blood, and my brother has now reduced his ambitious schemes to a redress of grievances, and change of bad ministers, particularly since you have joined your efforts to mine; for I have observed, since yesterday's conference, that he is more than ever disposed to follow my advice, and submit himself to our offended father on the conditions I have mentioned. Your own conduct proves that you were wearied and indignant at the confinement in the valley; we intend to exact from our father a promise that no son of Abissinia shall be again reduced to that state of restraint and inaction, and to entreat that he will bestow on us employments, of which we may without vanity declare ourselves to be more worthy than the indolent and pernicious ministers by whom he is surrounded. My desire is that you will join us in this request; you are less odious to our father, and may more easily prevail: if you persist in refusing an union so necessary to our general welfare, even should conquest smile on your arms, you will have not only the remorse of having destroyed your brothers, but will expose yourself to the artful snares and malicious envy of a court: your triumph will be short, and your ruin certain."

"Brother!" replied the prince, "I wish we could with justice say that blood has been spared – have you forgotten the death of Zengis? I am grieved to be compelled to reproach you with it; but should be far more grieved were my future life to be poisoned with a like reproach: yet mine would be the crime of necessity; yours has been that of choice.

"I hope, Menas, thou dost not even thyself suspect me of being capable of accepting thy proposals; my father can have no worse ministers than rebels; and were I to persuade him to receive you into his councils, I should render myself an accomplice of your crime. If you will return to your duty, your submission must be unconditional, and so will be your pardon: I trust these considerations may have their due weight: to-morrow's conference, or to-morrow's battle, decides your destiny."

Rasselas said no more, but commanded his guards to conduct the prince in safety to his tents.

Chapter 24

VICTORY AND GRATITUDE TO THE CONQUEROR

THE NEXT MORNING, by break of day, the two armies appeared as before, drawn up in order of battle, and the conference was resumed.

Menas, who had reason, from the firmness he observed in Rasselas, to apprehend that a general engagement would not be favourable to the rebels, had by this time changed his opinion, or at least wished to amuse[26] his brother with the prospect of a reconciliation; but Sarza's impetuosity now took place of his returning affection: he broke the conference, gave the signal of battle, and scarcely left Rasselas time to set himself at the head of his army before he attacked him with impetuosity.

The prince defended himself with intrepidity and skill, and his troops better disciplined, though inferior in number to the enemy, seconded his wishes: he had particularly commanded his soldiers to spare the lives of the princes. Sarza was taken prisoner, but Menas escaped by flight: a part of the army surrendered, and the rest were dispersed.

Rasselas returned to Gonthar, and laid the trophies of victory at his father's feet: he with difficulty obtained the pardon of Sarza, whom the emperor had resolved to sacrifice to his resentment, or rather to the counsels of his ministers. At length, in consideration of the services and supplications of Rasselas, he decreed that Sarza should return to the happy valley, accompanied by a strong guard, by which he was to be continually surrounded.

The emperor then took the diadem from his head, and would have placed it on that of Rasselas, but the prince resolutely refused to accept it, and declared his intention of retiring to the happy valley, whence he would never more depart, except by the express commands of the emperor, and in the greatest exigencies of the state.

The emperor at first combated his resolution with gratitude and

---

[26]*amuse*: "To keep in expectation" (in order to gain or waste time: OED).

tenderness, but finding Rasselas steady in his determination, and attending himself to the representations of his favourites, who were not sorry for the prince's departure, he at length consented to his retreat, loading him with riches and honours.

Rasselas, before he departed, gave his father an account of Imlac and the astronomer, and desired that they might be permitted to accompany his sister and her attendant to the happy valley.

He recommended Amalphis to the emperor, who promised to reward his services: he likewise informed him of his own engagement with Zilia, requesting permission to conclude a marriage, which, though contrary to the custom of Abissinia, might be authorised by the approbation of the emperor, and would add happiness to his retirement. To this he obtained no other answer than vague promises of compliance, when the troubles of the state should be perfectly appeased, which promises his father never meant to fulfil.

By the unaccountable desire of secrecy in matters of no avail, which forms all the policy of weak governments, assisted by the invisibility of despotic princes and their families, the person and history of Rasselas were unknown, though his actions could not be concealed. It was generally understood in Abissinia, that one of the king's sons had headed the army and gained a decisive victory; that he was to return to the happy valley, whence they supposed he had been taken for the conduct of the war; but no more was known, and no further enquiries were made.

Rasselas however received from his troops the most sincere testimonies of affection and regret. The man who has shared the dangers of his general in the field, is neither ignorant of his true character, nor will be silent on a subject so interesting to his own honour. The soldiers idolized the valour, and respected the prudence of Rasselas, and even declared they could not serve under another commander, after having followed the orders of their beloved prince.

Chapter 25

RETROSPECT OF A LIFE OF DISSIPATION

THE PRINCE WISHED to make a visit to the fortress before he devoted himself to lasting seclusion; but the emperor having expressed a desire that he would lose no time to accompany his brother Sarza, who was considered as a prisoner of state, he departed from Gonthar, and soon arrived at the happy valley.

It is difficult to express the sentiments of Rasselas when the massy gates, which separate the valley from the rest of the universe, closed behind him. Amalphis and his son, Imlac, the astronomer, and Nekayah, but above the rest Zilia, presented themselves forcibly to his mind: he found as much resolution was necessary in this moment, as when he thought himself condemned to perish unknown in the Arabian tower. He sought the palace, and had the additional mortification of finding that neither his victory nor his obedience received the praise which they deserved; that his return was considered as an act of compulsion, and that curiosity and suspicion alone brought society around him.

But, supported by the sentiment of conscious virtue, he looked on all his sufferings as so many additions to his triumph: that effort which impels to great actions, or painful sacrifices, continues awhile to support the mind with a sort of elastic force; but time diminishes the communicated vigour, and it falls again into dejection and languor. Such was the state of Rasselas, who no longer found himself weary alone of the happy valley, but weary of his existence. Indifferent to instruction, and insensible to hope, he wandered in solitude without enjoying the beauties of nature, and returned to the palace without admiring the works of art.

His melancholy was increased by the despair of Sarza. A gloomy horror had taken the place of ambition in the heart of this mistaken prince: he found he had been misled by those whom he had most trusted, and regarded Rasselas in no other light than as a conqueror. Shame and anger made him reject the consolations of a brother, who now feeling no other sentiments for him but those of tenderness and compassion, endeavoured, with unremitting solicitude, to soften the impressions of his grief, and the violence of his resentments.

The efforts of Rasselas were long fruitless. He had the pain of seeing that Sarza's impatience of his fate brought on him a gradual decay. As his health wasted, Rasselas became still more assiduous to console him: he soon gave up his whole time to this employment, and found in it a mournful satisfaction that compensated the mortifications he endured. Whenever he perceived in Sarza the least sensibility of his attentions, a heartfelt pleasure repaid him for his anxiety, and he began to thank Heaven for having placed him in a situation to assist his brother.

His mind now enjoyed more tranquillity, when he was one day surprised with the joyful intelligence of the arrival of Nekayah, who, as all danger of war seemed to be past, was, by the emperor's command, taken from the fortress, and conducted to her former habitation. Imlac accompanied her, and the astronomer obtained permission to follow them.

After the first transports of their meeting had subsided, Rasselas enquired anxiously after Zilia and her father. "I fear," said he, "that the letters which I have sent to the fortress must have been intercepted at Gonthar, as none of my messengers have ever returned. What must have been the ideas of Zilia; and what must the good Amalphis now think of me?"

"I was myself," answered the princess, "in the greatest uneasiness. Our information of the events of the war was confused and uncertain: we were kept in the most painful agitation by a variety of reports; and the messenger, who brought the emperor's orders for my return to the valley, was the first who acquainted us with the true state of affairs; at the same time he delivered to me new injunctions of secrecy in regard to our condition,[27] and I had not even the consolation of informing Amalphis and Zilia of the place destined for my habitation, nor of the situation of my brother: all I could tell them in answer to their frequent enquiries was, that I knew you followed the fortunes of the prince, who had commanded the royal army, and that I would give them the speediest intelligence in my power."

The first days of the re-union of Rasselas and Nekayah passed in

---

[27]*condition*: "Rank."

these mutual narrations, and in various fruitless endeavours to dispatch some messenger with letters to the fortress. Imlac returned to his studies, and the astronomer was delighted with the splendor and novelty of the scene. Pekuah was liberal in her communication to the inhabitants of the valley, and was soon surrounded by a numerous auditory. The prince and princess found their concern lessened by reciprocal confidence; they joined their efforts for the assistance and consolation of Sarza, whose health grew every day more precarious: as his strength decreased, his passions softened; he seemed no longer to regret the ill success of his enterprize, but to repent that he had attempted it. He confessed to Rasselas how artfully he had been led astray by the insinuations of Menas, and perceiving the resources which Rasselas and Nekayah found in literary pursuits and innocent pleasures, he regretted not having followed the same path, and tenderly acknowledged their kindness to him.

"Alas!" said he, one day, when they had drawn his sofa to the window of the apartment, where he was confined, "why have I been hitherto insensible to the beauties of nature? Yon vast orb of light, which tinges with the brightest purple the exhalations that accompany its retreat, is new to Sarza! If I have ever watched its disappearing, it has been only as a signal to the commencing banquet, in the hopes of tumultuous pleasures; nor has its rising majesty impressed on me other images than those of disgust, as it warned me to retire from the scene of riot, and intoxication. How often have I repined at the appearance of yon silvery moon, which attracts the enraptured eyes of Nekayah as it advances to take possession of the sky, and yield us a more gentle light to compensate the splendor we have lost: I feared its rays, lest they should betray my disguise, and force me to return guiltless.

"O Rasselas! O Nekayah! you have not always been happy, but you know not the pangs of remorse: you are unacquainted with the horrors of guilt: I have not one consolatory reflection to soften my last moments; nothing remains on my mind but confused scenes of dissipation, of intemperance, of error, at best of folly! Among those whom similar pursuits and base adulation made my companions, not one can I call by the sacred name of friend, not one whose breast will feel for me the tender pang of pity, or whose bleeding heart sympathizes with mine. – Chimerical dreams of criminal ambition had taken possession of my serious moments, and lawless revelling was all my gaiety. – It is over, and my tardy repentance only consecrates to virtue, to reason, and to affection, the hours of pain, of disappointment, and of satiety.

"The bleeding form of the unhappy Zengis is ever present to my imagination! – yet why should I say unhappy? He whose talents I depreciated, and whose mildness I despised, is now superior to me; for he died innocent, and I am his murderer! My father's stern indifference stings me to the soul – even thou, Rasselas, whose tender care sooths my affliction, thou excitest in me a sentiment of grief and remorse; why did I not listen to thee sooner! – Of Menas I cannot think without horror, and, condemn me not while I speak it, scarcely without detestation. – I endeavour to forgive him; but how far am I yet from attaining that resignation and serenity with which thou seekest to inspire me!"

Nekayah remained in tears, during the discourse of Sarza, and Rasselas strove to calm his agitated mind with hopes for the future, and consolations for the past.

"Thou art not the first, my brother," said he, "whom violent passion and smooth seduction have led into error; the same qualities, which raise to the height of heroism, may, when wrong directed, lead us to the precipice of guilt; but repentance is always in our power, nor are the means wanting for thee to retrieve the virtue thou hast lost: rash ambition, and immoderate love of pleasure may make us commit faults, nay even crimes; but dissimulation, perfidy, and cowardice are the only vices that render honour irretrievable: I know thou hast not descended to any of these; they are contrary to thy nature; thy virtues are thy own, thy errors proceed from others, and more than all, from the dreadful fatality that attends greatness."

Chapter 26

A NEW INHABITANT ENTERS THE VALLEY

WHILE THE PRINCES and Nekayah were thus employed a messenger entered, and informed them that Menas was returned to court, and reinstated in the emperor's favour: by secret correspondence with his father's ministers, from the place of his retreat, he had found means to clear himself from the imputation of any share in the rebellion, by throwing the whole blame on Sarza, and now governed Abissinia in the name of the emperor. Insinuations had been given that the interviews between Rasselas and Sarza were frequent, and consequently seditious; the emperor's age and natural temper inclined him to suspicion, and some officers of the army, who were friends to Rasselas, had dispatched this messenger to conjure him to be on his guard.

This intelligence, however kind, was useless; it was immediately followed by a mandate from court, which ordered Rasselas to one of the towers of the palace, whence it was not permitted him to have any communication with his brother.

Nekayah divided her time between her two brothers, but she had not long occasion to shew her tenderness to Sarza; this last stroke hastened his end, and he expired soon after in the arms of his sister, resigned and repentant.

In the mean time the successful Menas, not contented with having in his hands the sole authority in Abissinia, wished to have it confirmed by the name and honours of royalty: he endeavoured to persuade his father to retire to the happy valley, and pass the remainder of his life in ease and tranquillity; but the emperor was unwilling to inhabit a place, that offered him nothing but the image of death or of rebellion, and had even avoided making his annual visit: besides, he had been long accustomed to royalty, and feared dependence. Danger had engaged him to offer the resignation of his throne to Rasselas; that motive was no more, and his refusal to Menas was accompanied with severe reproach.

But the emperor only retained the exterior of royalty; the power had passed from his feeble hand into the grasp of Menas: his anger was therefore derided, and his remonstrances were neglected; and finding, with grief, that the only means to retain the poor appearance of sovereignty, was to consent unconditionally to the desire of his son, he took the road of the valley, surrounded by every new professor of the arts of luxury whom he could collect, seeking to forget the power he had lost in scenes of magnificence and pleasures.

Menas, being thus arrived at the summit of his wishes, was yet disturbed with doubts and alarms: he feared his father would forget the prejudices with which he had inspired him against Rasselas, and that duty as well as allegiance might induce the latter to make a desperate effort to replace him on the throne: to prevent therefore all communication which could awaken in the emperor his former affection for Rasselas, he insinuated to him, that the visits which the prince received from his sister and friends, were dangerous to the peace of Abissinia, and that the only effectual means of preventing the ill consequences that were likely to ensue from their meetings, was to secure every individual of the party.

The emperor approved, or at least consented to this proposal. Imlac and the astronomer were condemned to separate confinements, and the princess with difficulty obtained permission to be attended by her favourite Pekuah in the apartments which were assigned her as a prison.

The artful Menas had no sooner effected his designs, than he sought every means for rendering the retirement of his father a magnificent and seducing prison: he sent frequent messengers with superb presents, accompanied by the most skilful artists, and by all those who make it their study to delight; his letters were filled with expressions of filial duty, complaints of the fatigue of government, and suspicions cautiously introduced of seditions excited by emissaries of Rasselas.

Sumptuous banquets, the charms of poetry and music, ease and flattery, took such strong possession of the aged emperor, that at length he considered his retreat as a shelter from the storms of life, and gave the strictest orders for guarding Rasselas and the princess, lest they should endeavour to disturb his repose.

Much time passed in this manner: the prince made many daring but fruitless attempts to recover his liberty, and to convince his father of the fatal error into which he had fallen: the princess was not more successful in her endeavours.

Imlac made use of the lessons of philosophy, which he had learned in the experience of a long life, and comforted himself with reflecting, that revolutions are frequent in eastern monarchies. He was, however, uneasy with respect to the astronomer: he feared that solitude might again pervert his imagination, and bring back those ideas, with which it had formerly been led astray:[28] he therefore sought, and at last obtained permission of his guards to be removed to the same prison, and soon perceived that his fears had not been groundless. The astronomer confessed to Imlac, that he had been seized with a hopeless melancholy, in which he considered his imprisonment as a punishment for having neglected, in the charms of conversation, the great charge of the government of the seasons: the reason and eloquence of Imlac soon convinced him of his error, but could scarcely console him for the privation of general society. "I feel," said he, "that pleasure and amusement are natural to the mind of man: curiosity incites us to engage in the busy scenes of life; they who have not enjoyed them in youth will seek them in age, with that avidity which naturally attends on every wish, whose gratification has been long delayed. Age has fewer resources, and consequently stands more in need of the assistance of others: study becomes difficult, and therefore irksome: hope is less extensive, and gives less consolation: the moments appear to us more precious as we suppose them to be fewer, and we fear to retreat for an instant, lest we should be totally laid aside."

---

[28]See *Rasselas*, chapters 41-43.

Chapter 27

RETURN OF A FRIEND

NEKAYAH, WHO had at present more time for reflection than she had ever before experienced, passed her days in a less uneasy manner than any of the other captives. She was persuaded that happiness was unattainable, and this persuasion, which is perhaps destructive to the fortunate, is often useful to the unhappy: the attachment of Pekuah was a consolation, but she depended more on herself than on others. Compelled to renounce what she most loved, no other companion could be an adequate compensation; she was devoid of hope and of fear, and having experienced their vicissitudes, she felt the advantages of tranquillity.

One day Pekuah informed her that she had perceived, during many successive evenings, a young man of lofty stature, and generous[29] aspect, though poorly clothed, who soon after sun-set took his post opposite to her windows, and seemed to desire to be noticed, but that fear of the guards had always prevented her from gratifying her curiosity of knowing his intentions; that for a while he had been absent, but that she had seen him again the preceding evening.

Nekayah ordered her to observe, and if he returned that night, make signs to him to come round to the eastern side of their mansion, as it overlooked the lake; and endeavour to make him comprehend, that he might approach near enough in a boat to converse unobserved. "It is probably," added Nekayah, "some messenger from my brother, and if my conference with him can afford Rasselas comfort, I would neglect nothing to facilitate his access."

The young man did not appear that evening; but on the following night, as the princess and Pekuah were looking over from a terrace near the lake, they perceived a small boat advancing towards them, and soon after saw two persons leap on shore and silently climb the ascent that led to the castle; one of them placed a ladder against the

---

[29]*generous*: "Not of mean birth; of good extraction."

terrace wall, and mounted with rapidity, not without alarming the princess and Pekuah. The stranger soon put an end to their fears, by discovering himself to be the messenger whom they had formerly dispatched from the fortress to the court of Abissinia, and who had since been retained for his musical talents in the train of the old emperor. The princess, delighted with seeing him, was about to ask him various questions, when he informed her that no time was to be lost, that the son of Amalphis was beneath the terrace, and desired permission to visit her, as he had something of importance to communicate.

Nekayah's joy and agitation were greater than any language can express, and she had scarcely recovered the power of utterance when Dinarbas appeared disguised in the habit of a fisherman.

After the first emotion natural to their situation was subsided, he informed her, that he had long attempted in vain to approach her apartment, and had been equally unsuccessful in his endeavours to speak with Rasselas; that at last he had the good fortune of meeting the messenger, who told him on which side the palace was most accessible, and accompanied him in a boat, which he had procured: "I am now," added Dinarbas, "come to offer you my assistance, and I am rejoiced that fortune has so singularly distinguished me, as to put it in my power, perhaps, to free you and the prince from your confinement: O Nekayah! we may yet be happy – "

He was going to proceed in his narrative, when the hour approaching to relieve the guard, Nekayah warned him to retire, lest the boat should be observed. Dinarbas obeyed, with a promise of returning the next evening.

Chapter 28

ADVENTURES OF DINARBAS

DINARBAS, CHARMED with having seen Nekayah, persuaded the messenger to accompany him to the tower where Rasselas was confined, and, if possible, procure his admittance: the attempt was successful, and what neither the prince nor his friend could have effected, however penetrative and active were their minds, the slave, accustomed to combine and to employ stratagems, easily accomplished.

The prince and Dinarbas embraced each other with equal joy, and mutual demonstrations of friendship: as the latter had entered unperceived, they found sufficient opportunity for conversation; and the son of Amalphis related to Rasselas all that had passed since his quitting the fortress in search of him.

"I sought for you long in Egypt," said he, "and afterwards in Arabia, where, on the frontiers, I met a party of Arabs, who told me they had seen you under the guard of Turkish horsemen, and supposed that you were gone to Constantinople. I could not hear of your embarkation at Cairo, but continued my voyage in hopes of finding you at the court of the sultan. As that prince had shewn openly his disapprobation of the conduct of the late Bassa of Cairo, he was singularly desirous of paying every attention possible to the Abissinian nation: he had heard my name, and had approved my actions; he received me with peculiar courtesy: he commanded that diligent search should be made after the prisoner for whom I was come to supplicate his justice, and named a day on which I was to return to know the result of his enquiries. His enquiries were fruitless; but he told me, that he was not placed on the throne of Mahomet to abandon the innocent, or to favour injustice; that many Greek pirates had lately infested the seas in his dominions, and that as it was probable they might have intercepted the Turks, with my friend, in their passage from Cairo to Constantinople, he had given orders for strictly searching all the Greek islands and the coasts of that country: in the mean while he desired me to remain at his court, and held various discourses with me on the art of war: he listened to my answers with attention and complacency,[30] and discovered much of the genius and knowledge for which he has been so justly celebrated in his transactions with the Venetians. During my interviews with him, I found how unjustly we often attribute to greatness fastidious[31] and oppressive insolence: he who finds himself by birth superior in rank to the rest of mankind, can have neither the motives of jealousy, nor of emulation; his condescension will scarcely be abused, or his courtesy humiliated: it is not so with him who has risen above his equals by the caprice of fortune, and whose ambition makes him still aim at loftier distinctions: he fears lest affability and ease should again sink him to his former station; and as his greatness is only comparative, he thinks himself obliged to support it by artificial means. Whatever qualities may be wanting in sovereigns, courtesy is, I believe, rarely among the number; but this is not a time to lengthen my story with reflections.

"Before the vessels returned, which the sultan had ineffectually sent in quest of you, I had sufficiently gained his confidence to obtain permission to undertake the same expedition with my Abissinians. He granted me a light armed galley, skilful mariners, and an experienced pilot: with these I visited not only the islands, but great part of the continent belonging to the dominions of the sultan."[32]

---

[30]*complacency*: "Pleasure; satisfaction"; "Civility."
[31]*fastidious*: "Disdainful."
[32]Most of Greece was part of the Turkish Empire from 1456 to 1829.

Chapter 29

ADVENTURES OF DINARBAS CONTINUED

HERE RASSELAS exclaimed, "How often have I wished to view those places celebrated in history, and sung by the poets of antiquity!"

"Prince," replied his friend, "your leisure moments may hereafter be employed in listening to the incidents of my travels; at present, both your curiosity and your interest must require me to hasten to a conclusion of the narrative. Not finding my attempts successful, I directed my galley towards Candia, where the fleet and army of the sultan, under the command of the grand vizier, had been long employed against the united forces of the western world, who assisted the Venetians, in maintaining a siege of more than two years.[33] As I had now lost all hopes of finding my prince, I wished at least to testify my sense of the sultan's goodness to me: I happened fortunately to arrive on the eve of the day allotted for the general attack of the place: I obtained permission of the vizier to head a considerable body of troops, and had the good fortune to carry the bastion of Sant' Andrea, one of the most important of the city: much of the success of the assault was attributed to this action: I was loaded with praises by the vizier, and advanced to the highest commands. The place capitulated soon after, and our army returned triumphant to Adrianople, where the sultan then was, and where the peace, for which the Venetians were obliged to sue, the mortification of the haughty princes of Europe, and the despair of the chief of their religion, added new glories to the victory of the sultan. His munificence was proportioned to his successes; he considered my services as the most signal, perhaps because they were voluntary; he recompensed me with sovereignty; and to retain me in his dominions,

---

[33]Candia (modern Herakleion), chief port of Crete, was besieged by the Turks for over 20 years; in 1667, the grand vizier Ahmed Kiuprili took command and in September 1669 ousted the Venetians (who had controlled Crete for four centuries) and their French and other allies.

made me despot of Servia:[34] my kingdom is only dependent on the sultan, so far as I am obliged to assist his allies, and attack his enemies; and I have the next place to the grand vizier in the divan. At Adrianople I heard of your victory over your brothers, and of your retreat into this valley. The promise which I had given Nekayah would not allow me to disclose your history to the sultan; but after I had made a visit to my new dominions, I found him, at my return to his court, interested in your favour, and received from him the account of your imprisonment, and of the intrigues of Menas against you, of the forced retirement of the emperor from public business, and the death of Sarza. I was surprized to see the facility with which sovereigns can penetrate into the most secret councils of neighbouring states, and the care they take to inform themselves of affairs with which they have no apparent connexion; while those who are deeply concerned in them are often blindly ignorant of the most essential circumstances. The opportunity was favourable to me, and I entreated permission of the monarch to go as his ambassador to Menas, and to employ his mediation as an ally, to demand the restoration of the emperor. He readily granted my request; but Menas returned me such specious answers, and gave so many apparent proofs of the voluntary retirement of your father, that I wrote to the sultan for leave to enter the valley, and there, by discoursing with our sovereign in the sultan's name, discover his real sentiments. I left my train at the fortress commanded by my father, where I am still supposed to remain with them; and disguising myself, found means to enter the valley with one of the messengers dispatched from court with presents to the emperor; but I have not yet been able to obtain access to him."

---

[34]Servia (modern Serbia), part of Yugoslavia for most of the 20th century, was part of the Turkish empire from the mid 15th century until 1815, though at times in the 18th century Austria gained control.

Chapter 30

DINARBAS VISITS THE EMPEROR

RASSELAS CONGRATULATED Dinarbas on his success at the court of the sultan, and thanked him for the offers of his assistance: "I fear," said he, "the emperor will not be prevailed on to replace himself on the throne: he seems immersed in pleasure and insensibility: he fears to think, and all means are taken to prevent his being undeceived. I am alarmed at the rashness of your attempt. The valley is filled with emissaries of Menas; and should you be discovered, you are lost."

"I have no fears of that sort," replied Dinarbas; "the sultan is not of a character to suffer tamely an injury to his ambassador; nor is Menas hardy enough to awaken his anger. Instruct me how I can obtain an audience of your father, and I have great hopes for the rest."

"First tell me," said Rasselas, "whether Amalphis and Zilia still remember me: I have experienced too many of the caprices of fortune to be anxious after the projects of ambition, and have found that the only ornament of prosperity, and the only consolation in adversity, is the sympathy of friendship and affection."

"They were totally ignorant of your fate," said Dinarbas, "and their anxiety was greater than I can describe. As I was not at liberty to discover to them the whole of your situation, I told them I had heard of your distinguishing yourself during the war; and that I believed you to be at present confined, by the order of Menas, in the happy valley. I promised them, at my departure, that they should soon receive fuller information. Let us now consider what methods will prevail with the emperor."

"I know not," said Rasselas, "whether we shall render him a service in tearing the veil which Menas has so artfully drawn around him; and I doubt not that, if he were replaced on the throne, he would regret the delights of the happy valley: all I can wish from your friendship is, that you will endeavour to convince him of my innocence, and of that of Nekayah; and I know no easier nor safer means of admittance than to proclaim yourself the son of Amalphis: the fidelity of your father is well known to the emperor, and he will sooner admit a subject, than the ambassador of a powerful neighbour."

"Pardon me, prince," answered Dinarbas, "if I say that you judge the emperor by your own heart: power could not dictate to you, but fidelity might soothe you: I will however try the expedient which you propose, but if it succeeds, I know not the character of the emperor."

Dinarbas staid till the shades of night permitted him to depart unperceived: he then left the prison of Rasselas, and went to the terrace, where he was again received by Nekayah and Pekuah: he related to them his adventures and his intentions. The princess charged him not to discover himself as ambassador from the sultan, till he had sounded the disposition of her father: "I know," said she, "that the spirit of an emperor of Abissinia can never brook the interference of a foreign power."

Dinarbas, against his own inclinations, obeyed the counsel of the prince and princess: he announced himself to the emperor as the son of Amalphis, who had important affairs to communicate. The sovereign gave for answer, that he must apply to Menas; but recollecting himself that Nekayah and Rasselas had been long under the guard of Amalphis, he concluded the son might be accomplice of their supposed crimes, and commanded him to enter, surrounded with guards.

Dinarbas then related with frankness and energy, all the circumstances of the wrong done to Rasselas and the princess: he spared not Menas as an usurper; and invited the emperor to return to his throne, and do justice to his family; but his discourse made no other impression on the monarch than to convince him that Rasselas must have been guilty, as he had betrayed the secret of his birth, and that the son of Amalphis was his accomplice. As Dinarbas could not exculpate the prince without accusing Nekayah, he blushed, and was embarrassed.

The emperor considered this as a signal of guilt, and commanded him instantly to be imprisoned.

Dinarbas now thought himself at liberty to act upon his own plan: he declared himself ambassador from the sultan, sent by him in the most open manner to remonstrate with Menas, and, should he not succeed with him, to apply to the emperor, assure him of the sultan's friendship, and reinstate him on the throne.

Awe of superior power took place of anger in the heart of the sovereign: he knew not what he was to believe; but he resolved to send a messenger to his son for instructions, and in the mean time to treat Dinarbas with the respect due to the representative of the sultan.

A report was spread next day in the valley, by messengers arrived from Gonthar, that a considerable body of Turkish troops had marched towards the frontiers of Abissinia. This news engaged the emperor to pay still more attention to Dinarbas, and even to grant the request he made of visiting Rasselas as often as he should think proper.

Chapter 31

SKETCH OF THE TRAVELS OF DINARBAS

DINARBAS FORBORE to make any remarks to the prince on the conduct of the emperor: he simply related to him what had passed; from which Rasselas formed small hopes: he found that his friend was in some sort become, on his account, a prisoner of state, and he was alarmed at his danger.

"Fear not for me," said Dinarbas, "I know my steps are watched, and that I must remain here till the emperor hears from Menas; but I hope by that time to have convinced him of your innocence, and of the necessity of his returning to the management of public affairs: no sovereign, I believe, ever retired but by some species of constraint; and none, I am convinced, ever failed of repenting the step he had taken. Authority and active life are too natural to the mind, not to retain their hold, however circumstances may have at any period weakened their impression: the scenes of action will retrace themselves to the voluptuary in the bosom of pleasure, and to the anchorite in the cell of austerity. When the emperor reflects on the conversation I held with him last night, he will find the charms of royalty again rush on his imagination, and with a few more interviews, I hope to rouse all his sleeping ambition."

Rasselas found his imprisonment greatly relieved by the visits of Dinarbas, who every day informed him of the progress he made with the emperor, in awakening his tenderness for the prince and princess. Rasselas however did not willingly give way to hope, and would often change the subject of conversation, by asking Dinarbas for the detail of his travels in the dominions of the sultan.

"I have often wished to know," said Rasselas, "whether the scenes so beautifully described by the ancient European poets are really as interesting as we should believe from their works, did we not judge by our own writers of the embellishments of poetry. I have always considered our total ignorance of other countries as one of the greatest misfortunes that attends our government, and have tried to obviate this inconvenience for myself, as far as books could assist me."

"In my voyages in the Archipelago and Mediterranean," replied Dinarbas, "I have seen enough to solve your question: nations have disappeared from the face of the earth, laws have been forgotten, and morals corrupted; but nature, though subject to great revolutions, ever remains beautiful in temperate climates. That poets have been thought to embellish nature is an opinion that must have had its rise and its continuance in countries where the northern blasts deface the charms of fertility, or where the too ardent rays of the sun dry up its sources; but in those happy climes where vegetation is never wholly stopped, poets will be found, with all their eloquence, to trace very faintly the charms of nature. The Abissinian, scorched on the burning sands that surround him; the Scythian, sliding over frozen rivers, and climbing mountains, whose dazzling whiteness makes no distinction to the sight, can have but a very imperfect idea of the variegated landscape that attracts the eyes of the fortunate inhabitant of Greece.

"In these celebrated scenes every thing tends to diversify and heighten the beauties of the prospect: The majestic rocks, glowing with all the warmth of colouring; the cascades, reflecting the azure of an unsullied sky; the trees, not more various in their forms than in their hues; the earth, enriched with vegetable production: but chiefly that light and transparent vapour, which gives the faint blue to the distant mountains, and the splendid purple to the western clouds; and, like tenderness in moral life, softens every object, and diffuses serenity and rapture! Rasselas, thou mayest think me an enthusiast;[35] yet, hadst thou accompanied me in the enchanted spots where I have sought thee, thou wouldst have felt the same warmth of fancy, the same sensibility of heart that transported me: these are the favourite theatres of august and pleasing meditation. How often have I been led to adore the goodness of the Creator of the Universe, when wandering through some delightful valley, adorned as I have in vain attempted to describe to thee, I contemplated the beauties which he has so bountifully offered to man! There some majestic and awful ruin would rear its venerable head, and silently instruct me: every part in these countries unites the charms of situation and of celebrity; no mountain is without a name – the ground we tread is consecrated to fame in the historic page; even fable becomes respected, and while

---

[35]*enthusiast*: "One of a hot imagination, or violent passion"; "One of elevated fancy."

our heart is raised to heroism at the pass of Thermopylæ,[36] our imagination is filled with poetic ardour on the side of Olympus and Parnassus! In these places, the images of those who were most dear to me, returned with double force; I longed for my father amidst the ruins of Sparta, and for my prince near the temple of Theseus![37] In the shade of those trees, which are the progeny of the academic grove, I wished for the assistance of Imlac to converse with Plato and his disciples! My warlike companions were present to my thoughts at Platea,[38] and at Marathon.[39] In the valley of Tempé[40] I forgot, for a moment, my hopeless situation, and imagined that I saw Nekayah beside me, the humble and pleased companion of my enthusiastic raptures."

---

[36] Pass leading into Greece, where the Spartans lost a heroic battle against the Persians in 480 B.C.
[37] Best preserved Greek temple, near the Agora in Athens.
[38] Ancient Greek city where the Greeks defeated the Persians in 479 B.C.
[39] Village and plain where the Greeks defeated the Persians in 490 B.C.
[40] Ruggedly beautiful river valley near Mount Olympus, celebrated by Virgil and other poets.

Chapter 32

GRANDEUR OF THE ANCIENTS

"THOU HAST NOW said enough," replied the prince, "to be considered as an enthusiast by the greater part of mankind, by those whose hearts are steeled, or whose heads are stupified by interest or gaiety: happily we are not heard by them in this prison, where, if our bodies are enclosed, our minds are at liberty; a privilege not always attainable in the world. But, to return to thy travels, hast thou observed many of those monuments of ancient grandeur and elegance, of which the few scattered remains afforded me such delight in Egypt?"

"The effect which those buildings produced on me," said Dinarbas, "is far superior to my powers of description: the noble simplicity of the Grecian temples, the elegance of their proportion, the harmony of the parts, and the majesty of the whole, give an impression of awe and of satisfaction, which no modern building affords. I have never yet been able to comprehend how the taste of any architect should be so strangely depraved, as to permit him to view unmoved those stately fabrics, and vainly imagine he could, by mean plans, disproportionate combinations, and glittering deformity, give delight to rational spectators: yet such artists have been found, and they have not wanted protectors. He, who built the mosque of Santa Sophia,[41] undoubtedly supposed he had raised an edifice that would show how far the elegance of the golden age, in which he lived, was superior to the barbarism of that which saw the elevation of the temple of Theseus. It has ever been the irremediable error of weak minds and degenerate nations, to substitute ornament for proportion, curious minuteness for majestic beauty, and heterogeneous variety for harmony and grace.

"Our spires, our turrets, and our many coloured roofs, are become odious to my eyes, since I have beheld simplicity and elegance on the desolate shores of Greece: nor did the architecture alone take

---

[41]Hagia Sophia, a magnificent Christian church in Constantinople, was converted to a mosque by the Turks in 1453; it is now a museum.

possession of my imagination; I found the same characteristic feature in all their remaining productions.[42] Their inscriptions are lofty, pure, and energetic, they seem only written to convey the meaning, and the flowers of eloquence spring naturally from the subject. Their statues, not writhed into distortion to catch the eye by forced contrasts, are simple and beauteous like nature itself, which they represent in the general effect, more than by descending into little peculiarities: every figure speaks to the heart; we confess the influence of the passion it breathes, or the respect it inspires. But, in the works of modern art, even among its best performances, our mind must have the labour of combining particulars, before we perceive the general effect: we approve or criticise ere we can feel, and therefore scarcely feel at all. When we contemplate the masterpieces of the ancients, our sentiments are immediately engaged, our imagination is interested, and the first impression must begin to weaken before we can descend to minute examination; yet even then we admire; we see that, as in a well-ordered kingdom, though some parts are inferior, they are in their place, and contribute to the beauty of the whole.

"Such, in the view of moral or political greatness, if we examine history, was the conduct of the illustrious men of ancient Greece and Rome: their enterprises were vast, and their minds capacious; they formed a comprehensive plan, and acted up to it. It is not by adding one little idea to another, that perfection is insensibly attained. Alexander had conceived his scheme for the conquest of the east, before he left his native Macedon; nor did Cæesar take the command in Gaul, without a previous design of becoming the first in the republic. I am not surprised at the policy of our courts, which usually excludes their subjects from all communication with the knowledge of Europe: in order to confine us to narrow views, to indolent magnificence, and, if I may so express it, to living by the day: this is the surest foundation for despotism: the mind being easily reduced to inactivity, when its flights are not allowed to go beyond a certain extent."

---

[42]Knight was devoted to Mediterranean landscape and to classical architecture and art objects. By the time she had finished *Dinarbas*, she had created a portfolio of some 1800 sketches and colored drawings mainly of such subjects (Elliott-Drake, 139, et passim).

"All this is true," said Rasselas, "yet I cannot see what the sovereign gains by debasing the faculties of his subjects: a good prince will be respected and beloved by a wise nation, and, what he can never rely on from a herd of willing slaves, will be sure of their fidelity: he will not be deserted at the first appearance of a foreign enemy, or domestic usurper, who, in our despotic governments, obtains the same tribute of obedience as the rightful monarch, because he has the same authority, that of terror. What else could have so calmly placed Menas on the throne, at the expence of his brother's life, and his father's sovereign dignity?"

Chapter 33

THE PRINCE AND PRINCESS ACCOMPANY THEIR FATHER TO GONTHAR

DINARBAS AT LENGTH prevailed on the emperor to visit Nekayah, whose innocence it was easy to prove, and whose tenderness and eloquence soon convinced him of the truth of Rasselas: after a short struggle between pride and paternal affection, the prince was justified and restored to liberty.

The difficulty now remained to force Menas to resign a throne in which he was supported by his own guilt and that of traitors, who must defend him because they were his accomplices. It was probable that with the assistance of Amalphis, and from the fame of Rasselas, the troops might have been engaged to declare for their former sovereign; but their officers had been changed, men devoted to Menas now commanded them, and it was not easy, in case they were disposed to second the efforts of Rasselas, to communicate any plan by which they might act, without exposing themselves to the fury of the reigning party, before they could have a chief to support them.

The authority of the sultan might be easily exerted: he had warmly offered his mediation; and what sovereign will not warmly offer his mediation in the differences of his less powerful neighbours? This disposition of the Turks gave pain to Rasselas: he would have preferred any other method of reinstating his father on the throne of his ancestors: but his disgust to foreign aid he soon found to be fruitless. The report of a Turkish army marching towards the frontiers had not been without foundation; and more certain accounts arrived of their having penetrated into the heart of Abissinia. It was said that Amalphis and his garrison, who were entreated to join them, remained neuter, but had not prevented the train of Dinarbas from following them; that Menas, at the head of his troops, was gone out to meet them, and that a decisive battle might soon be expected.

It was now time to act: Dinarbas obtained permission of the emperor to join the Turkish army, where his presence was necessary, to prevent many irregularities. The confusion was become general, and the valley was no longer strictly guarded: the emissaries of Menas began to pay their court to the emperor, and his party, and suffered them to enjoy all the liberty they desired.

Dinarbas hastily advanced towards Gonthar, near which place he had been told the two armies lay encamped. He hoped by intimidating Menas, to make him resign the crown, and, after replacing the emperor on the throne, to conduct the sultan's troops back to his dominions; but, on his approach, he was met by the principal officers of his train, and the chiefs of the army, with the head of Menas: they informed him of their victory, and of the flight of the usurper under a mean disguise, in which he was stopped and put to death. They invited the son of Amalphis to share their triumph, and decide the fate of the prisoners, among whom were the principal ministers and favourites of Menas.

Dinarbas, in consequence of the sultan's mandate, delivered to him by the chiefs, assumed the command of the army, entered Gonthar, and dispatched messengers to the happy valley, entreating the presence of the emperor and Rasselas.

The death of Menas made little impression on his father, but deeply affected Rasselas and Nekayah: they had, however, the consolation to reflect that they were innocent of his fate, and accompanied the emperor to Gonthar, attended by the lady Pekuah, Imlac, and the astronomer, whom they had restored to liberty, as soon as they were reinstated in the favour of their father.

Chapter 34

INCONVENIENCES OF FOREIGN AID

THE EMPEROR RESUMED with joy the imperial dignity, but made few reflections on the revolutions which replaced him on the throne; and, being asked what was to be done with his former favourites, he coolly ordered them to execution. Rasselas, however, obtained from him their pardon, on condition of their perpetual imprisonment, and the sovereign mentioned them no more.

He likewise complied with the request of Rasselas to send a messenger to the fortress of Amalphis, to demand Zilia in marriage. As she was the sister of his deliverer, whom he loaded with praises and thanks, he no longer considered the alliance as derogatory from his dignity. A train of women and slaves accompanied the messenger, to honour the royal bride; and letters from Rasselas, Nekayah, and Dinarbas, informed Amalphis and Zilia, that the prince and princess, formerly celebrated by fame for their sufferings, and now for a happy reverse, were the guests whose society they had enjoyed in the fortress. These letters contained a minute detail of all the public events, and the sentiments of Rasselas on his change of fortune. Amalphis was invited to court with a considerable command in the army.

Rasselas impatiently expected the arrival of Amalphis and Zilia, and in the mean time saw with grief the disorder which reigned in the capital and its environs, from the licence given by the officers of the Turkish army to their numerous troops. Dinarbas, though invested with the chief command, found it difficult to exercise severe authority over foreign soldiers elated with victory, conscious of belonging to superior power, and of having conferred assistance. The officers were haughty and extravagant in their demand, the men riotous and avaricious; the highways were infested by their outrages, nor were the houses of the inhabitants of the city protected from their lawless insolence. In vain did Dinarbas attempt, by alternate menaces and soothing, to reduce them to discipline; the timidity of the Abissinians had given them an advantage which they had no inclination to relinquish: a reinforcement was advancing from Egypt; the sultan, either not being yet informed of the success of the enterprize, or choosing to facilitate and give validity to a treaty of alliance with Abissinia, by the presence of a formidable army.

"Prince," said Dinarbas to his friend, "I am sensible that I have involved you in all the present difficulties, by rashly engaging the sultan in your interest: your doubts were justly founded, and I know not how to extricate you from the danger of which I have been inadvertently the cause. If I depart for the sultan's court to remonstrate with him on the conduct of his troops, I leave them without a chief to repress in any degree their excesses. I have written to entreat him to recall them, but I have no reason to hope, from the present appearance of things, that my request will be granted without a demand on his side, of concessions injurious to your honour."

"Dinarbas," answered the prince, "if we were to be accountable for the ill success of every good intention, we must suppose ourselves endued with general prescience, a quality inherent in the Divinity alone. Your proceedings were open and just, and you had no reason to imagine that the Turkish army would be lawless and ungenerous: we are not yet assured whether the sultan is in fault: if he is not, he will recall his troops; but if he persists in treating us like a conquered kingdom, we have a right to consider him as our enemy, not our benefactor; and his enmity is perhaps not so formidable as the world has been taught to suppose.

"By the accounts thou hast often given me of the siege of Candia, he owes that conquest more to the division of the enemy, and to the singular bravery of some of his officers, among whom thou hast been particularly distinguished, than to the general tenour of his conduct: it is even probable that all his efforts would have proved fruitless, had not the Venetians been abandoned by their allies. They who trust to the mutability of courts, and to the complicated interests of governments, will find themselves deserted like the Venetians, or menaced like ourselves. The only way to make allies useful, is to be respectable without them.

"Consider how a small island in the same seas, merely from the courage and conduct of its defenders, victoriously resisted the attacks of the most formidable and most numerous armies of the Turks, headed by their ablest generals.[43]

"I have not the hopes of forming instantaneously a well-disciplined army, but I have at least learned not to fear ungovernable multitudes; and if I am compelled to take up arms, I shall dread more the imputation of ingratitude than the power of the sultan."

---

[43]In 1565, Malta repulsed a massive attack by the Turkish army and navy.

Chapter 35

DEATH OF THE EMPEROR

THE EMPEROR DID NOT long survive his usurping son: he was, like many other men, solicitous for the events that might happen after his death, though he had been careless of what had been done in his lifetime: all wish to extend their influence beyond the grave, and few approach their end without making some reflections on their past existence. The mind of the emperor was less weakened by age, than enervated by indolence and pleasures: when infirmity obliged him to retire from dissipation, thought returned upon him more forcibly; his tenderness for Rasselas and Nekayah redoubled as he was about to quit them. "My children," said he, "I shall neither leave you precepts nor example; I can only beseech you to beware of my errors, and, if possible, to cast a veil over my faults – I have, by indolence, brought my kingdom into greater distresses, than the most cruel and avaricious tyrants have ever occasioned.

"I am now convinced that inactivity is generally the source of crime: it is scarcely possible for the man who does nothing to be free from guilt; we, in particular, are placed in a sphere, in which it is our duty to direct, like the pilot, who, if he neglects the rudder for an instant is in danger of seeing the vessel dashed on the neighbouring rock. Yet are not my faults without extenuation; a mistaken notion of humanity has made me detest war, and consequently neglect my army; the desire of being loved has induced me to court the friendship of my slaves, and you see the gratitude of my favourites: a mind not uninformed nor incurious led me naturally to the love of arts and sciences; but this inclination has been falsely turned to those of luxury and amusement, rather than to those of political or moral utility. Had I possessed sufficient energy of mind to rouse myself from the illusions that surrounded me, I might have seen the fallacy of my ideas as soon as I had attempted to investigate them; but the dream was prolonged by all who came near me; the vicious offered to me new schemes of dissipation, and even the virtuous praised me for that gentleness and good nature, which they celebrated as superior to the shining qualities of the conqueror. War is, undoubtedly, shocking to humanity; but while we live amongst mortals, actuated by mortal passions, we must be ever ready to defend those committed to our care.

"Thou, my son, to whom I am rather confessing my own errors than conveying instruction, hast the activity and rectitude which I have wanted. I believe that royalty will not shake thy virtues; yet consider how different is the state of the subject and the sovereign, the prince and the king. Thou wilt soon be absolute master of vast dominions; and, what is still more dangerous, master of thyself, with nothing to control, and every thing to mislead thee. Why is prosperity more dangerous than adversity? Because it leaves no obstacle to our will; because we have no restraint upon our passions, and, having no difficulties to struggle with, fall indolently asleep in the lap of pleasure. We often owe our preservation from final ruin to temporary evils. Mayest thou be preserved in dignity and honour by gentler means, by reason and virtue!"

Thus did the emperor lament the errors of his former conduct, and warn his son against the like misfortune. Rasselas received his exhortations with respect, and soon after, with tears of filial piety, saw his remains deposited in the tomb of his ancestors.

Chapter 36

REFLECTIONS OF RASSELAS ON HIS ACCESSION TO THE THRONE

RASSELAS WAS NOW, by right of succession, and with the general acclamations of the people, proclaimed emperor of Abissinia. He was not elated with the dignity; he looked round the sepulchral monuments of the royal house, and he could not, without a melancholy reflection, contemplate the tombs of a father and three brothers, who, in so short a space of time, had finished their course amidst the troubles in which the nation had been plunged.

"There," said he to Nekayah, from whom he was never separated, "there are the steps by which I have ascended the throne. O my sister! we are guiltless of these deaths, but let us be warned by the awful scene. Our Creator alone knows how many years, months, or days will revolve before we become inhabitants of this silent mansion; but as his goodness permits us a free agency in this life, let us endeavour to act so as to obtain more than a bare memorial that we have existed.

"Let us not entertain an impious vanity, because we have seen and avoided the errors of our race; let us offer up our thanks to Heaven for the greatest of all blessings, that of innocence. Born with the same frailties as those whose mortal remains fill these marble structures, we might, like them, have been the sport of contending passions, and at last the victims of their fury! We should now deserve execration, where they merited compassion, if with more instruction, with better friends, and especially with the knowledge of adversity, we had erred like them. Thou, Nekayah, hast a calm and serene part to act through life, and therefore less difficult than mine. Ye, whose ambitious wishes have long grasped at sovereign power, could you see the heart of Rasselas, you would fear to sink under the burden of cares and duties which it imposes on you.

"Nekayah! let us leave this scene of contemplation; not the dead but the living are to be benefited or injured by the sceptre of Rasselas: if to be injured, all-powerful arbitrator of mankind! let me soon hide my remorse, though not my shame, in some lone angle of this receptacle of death."

Having so said, he departed thoughtful. At the entrance of his palace, he met the chief of the slaves whom he had dispatched to the fortress. He anxiously enquired whether Zilia and Amalphis were arrived, and listened with the greatest agitation to the following answer.

"Dread Sovereign! when we were only at the distance of a day's journey from the fortress, the messenger who was charged with your letters suddenly disappeared: we searched for him long in vain; and, during this delay, received the news of our late emperor's death, and of your majesty's accession to the imperial power: we proceeded to the castle, where we related the purport of our mission, and the loss of our credentials: we informed the governor, of the various events which had contributed to place you on the throne; and we found he had long supposed you to be the same hero whose presence formerly honoured his mansion; but, how great was our surprise, when we perceived that, instead of complying with our request, he delivered to us this letter, and commanding us to assure the emperor of his inviolable fidelity, said he waited your further orders for prostrating himself at the foot of your throne!"

Chapter 37

LETTER OF ZILIA

RASSELAS FOUND the letter was from Zilia, and opened it with infinite impatience: it was conceived in these terms.

"As sincerity and candour are the ruling principles of Zilia, let my sovereign pardon me if I disclose my heart to Rasselas: think, O prince! what must be my sensations, when I learn that fortune and thy own merit have placed thee in a rank above my fondest hopes; and forgive me if I say, beyond my wishes. Had I at first inspired thee with that confidence which my heart tells me I deserve, I should not now be compelled to act a painful, and apparently an ungrateful part; but as thy prudence was then superior to thy passion, and as, since that time, every thing has prevented thee from conveying to me thy sentiments, an explanation is now necessary, both for thy satisfaction, and for my own.

"I thank thee for the assurance that thou wishest me to share thy honours; but does this wish arise from a scrupulous observance of thy promise, or from that affection which first dictated thy vows? The step thou hast taken is a proof of thy principles, but not of thy sentiments. Zilia could never doubt the honour of Rasselas; but is she assured of his love?

"Attend to me, O prince! The throne of Abissinia, even dignified as it is by thy virtues, has no charms for me, if the place which I once flattered myself with possessing in thy breast is no longer mine. Consult thyself; reflect whether the circumstances which constrained thee, during a time, to inhabit the fortress commanded by my father, did not favour an illusion: think whether, in the midst of the serious and important scenes in which thou hast been since engaged, the image of Zilia has invariably presented itself to thy memory. Hast thou the same sentiments from which we sometimes derived the highest felicity, and often the most anxious solicitude, when wandering beneath these lofty palm trees that overlook the plains of Abissinia, and the distant mountains whence the Nile derives its source, thou wouldst often say that joy, pleasure, and content were in this fortress, and all beyond its walls was a vast desert, or a troubled ocean? Was not this illusion, Rasselas? Hast thou not found in that desert, flowers not cultivated by the hand of Zilia; in that troubled ocean, harbours not formed by her care? In the midst of thy sufferings, hast thou wished to pour thy griefs into her faithful bosom? Hast thou at least thought her worthy of thy confidence?

"If the emotions of thy heart impelled thee to summon Zilia to the court of Gonthar, she will obey their summons; she will accept happiness and Rasselas; but if she owes this message to thy former promise, she will irrevocably resign herself to retirement, to distant admiration of thy virtues, and to prayers for thy prosperity: Rasselas, thou art free: whatever is thy answer, I know it will be dictated by truth, and received with gratitude."

It is impossible to describe the sensations with which Rasselas read this letter. Had his regard for Zilia suffered any change, it would have revived every tender thought; but the impression which her virtues had made on him, was not capable of diminution. He loved her with unabating fondness and unshaken constancy: he felt and applauded the delicacy of her sentiments, and immediately dispatched the same slaves to the fortress, with letters to Amalphis and Zilia that sufficiently assured them how necessary to his happiness was their speedy arrival. He took care that a stronger guard should accompany these attendants, as he supposed the defection of his messenger, during their former journey, must have been owing to some treacherous communication with the Turks: he had long seriously reflected on the ills which they occasioned, and resolved to make it his first care to free himself from these haughty allies.

Chapter 38

AMALPHIS ACCEPTS THE COMMAND OF THE TROOPS

RASSELAS SENT an ambassador to the sultan with letters, in which he returned him thanks for the assistance of his troops; requested the continuance of his friendship, but at the same time informed him, that, notwithstanding the care and diligence of Dinarbas, the insolence and irregularity of the officers and men were insufferable; and that his kingdom could not be at peace, till they were removed. He offered to defray all the expences of the war.

While Rasselas waited the answer of the sultan, he applied himself with unremitting vigilance to the forming of an army. He found many obstacles arising from the anarchy and confusion which had lately reigned in Abissinia: his former instructions were neglected; but he had not lost the affection of the troops; and what will not industry attain when assisted by power? He soon felt the salutary effects of his resolution. The Turkish army, intimidated by the improving forces of Rasselas, became more courteous and less rapacious; yet still he impatiently wished their removal from his dominions; fearing lest their want of discipline should infect his army, and their magnificence and luxury renew a desire for that splendour, which had been carried to the most reprehensible height during the reign of his father.

He was soon made happy by the arrival of Amalphis and Zilia. Convinced of the sentiments of Rasselas, she no longer hesitated to accompany her father to Gonthar. They were received amidst the acclamations of a people who considered the felicity of their sovereign as their own. A day was fixed for the celebration of the marriage, which was to take place immediately on the expiration of the first month's mourning for the late emperor. Dinarbas and Nekayah had a more particular share in the general joy. Rasselas willingly bestowed his sister on his friend and benefactor, and appointed the same time for their union.

He now told Amalphis that his intentions were to follow his counsels in all that regarded the military department, and conferred on him the supreme command in his army. "I cheerfully accept," said the venerable chief, "the employment with which my sovereign honours me, and I hope, by the performance of my duty, not to prove unworthy of such distinction; yet let not Rasselas follow blindly my counsels; let him consult his own reason, and that of other men who may have equal experience with myself, but who have not had the good fortune to be known to their sovereign. Who can flatter himself that he is devoid of partiality? I have, it is true, during my youth, lived much in extensive society; but in my age, confined to one spot, I must have naturally lessened my general experience in the discrimination of character, and may have fancied those around me most worthy of command, because my observation was confined to them alone. I feel, that when I seek for officers of merit, my thoughts will scarcely stray beyond my garrison; therefore I might not only commit injustice with respect to many of whose worth I am ignorant, but likewise do irreparable injury to your service, if I was to undertake the distribution of employments.

"This province more properly belongs to the sovereign, guided by the opinion of the nation, which he must study with unremitting diligence."

Chapter 39

RASSELAS TAKES A VIEW OF THE LEGISLATURE OF ABISSINIA

THE SULTAN SENT an ambassador to Rasselas in return; and, while he congratulated him on his accession to the throne, and promised to recall his forces, he proposed a treaty of alliance, the terms of which were highly injurious to the honour and interest of Abissinia. The sultan demanded, in virtue of this alliance, the cession of a considerable port in the Red Sea, which had long been the object of Turkish ambition, and was not only the greatest mart of Abissinian commerce, but the best safeguard of the coasts. This proposal had been made to the late emperor, who, by the intrigues of his ministers, was nearly led to accept it, in consideration of a large sum offered by the Turks, if he had not been timely prevented by the rebellion of his sons. The negotiation had been broken off, but a plea was still left for the sultan to renew it.

Rasselas received the ambassador with dignity, and answered him with firmness: he told him, he was not conscious of any obligations to the sultan which could authorize such demands; that he renounced all alliance that was not to be formed on a footing of equality; that he knew not what might have been his father's motive for entering into such negotiation; but that, in his situation, it would be no less abject than impolitic to become tributary to a man, whose assistance he had neither directly nor indirectly courted, and whose intentions, as they appeared from his demands, cancelled all obligation.

The ambassador had orders to denounce[44] war, in case of a refusal; but Dinarbas, who felt himself in some measure the cause of this dispute, and who, whatever might be the conduct of the sultan on this occasion, was attached to him by all the ties of honour, requested, and, though with difficulty, obtained permission of Rasselas to accompany the ambassador, and make a last attempt on the mind of his benefactor.

---

[44]*denounce*: "To threaten by proclamation."

Rasselas, in the mean time, with the assistance of Amalphis, prepared for war with an activity that alarmed the Turkish army, who remained within their camp, and seemed rather to fear being attacked, than to have any inclination to commence hostilities.

He did not neglect the civil part of government: he found the tribunals subject to injustice, the natural consequence of that dilatoriness which gives room for prejudice to bias the minds of those magistrates who have less penetration than study, while the greater number have not even the merit of endeavouring to distinguish right from wrong, but blindly fall in with the opinion of others to avoid the trouble of thinking for themselves. Rasselas took all possible means to obviate, in a temporary manner, these evils, by pardoning the condemned when there was the least probability of innocence; while he applied himself seriously, with the assistance of the most eminent for learning and rectitude, to form a code of laws, which might for the future rather prevent crimes than chastise them, and have equal power over the magistrate and the accused. This most arduous and most essential part of legislation at first alarmed him, on account of the labyrinths in which he found himself involved; yet, on examining the subject more closely, he believed it far less complex than he had first imagined. Virtue and vice, right and wrong, are, when truly considered, impossible to be mistaken: sophistry and prejudice may cast a veil over their features, but can not totally conceal them from him who seeks for justice and truth; and such was Rasselas. He therefore found few obstacles in framing laws for criminal judicature, and when he had once established them, he was firm to enforce their execution: their tenor was lenient, but it was impossible to escape from their power: he soon with pleasure perceived their efficacy, by an amazing diminution in the number of crimes committed in his dominions. At the same time, he found greater difficulties in forming a plan that might secure the possessions of his subjects from destructive chicanery, this part of justice being naturally involved in more perplexities, and less subject to evidence. Happily the Abissinians were not greatly addicted to these pursuits, which are rather the consequence of the degeneracy of a nation once civilized, than the remains of pristine barbarism; and Rasselas not only took care that testaments and laws should be as clear as possible, but discouraged every thing that tended to introduce litigious enquiries; and, being convinced that interest was generally the promoter of these mischiefs, he industriously placed magistrates in such a situation as to be, if possible, inaccessible to bribery; while, as the simplicity of the laws put it in the power of every man to plead for himself, there could be no exterior influence, such as he had observed in other countries, among the lower officers of justice, to breathe the flame of discord into weak minds from motives of interest and avarice.

Chapter 40

PRIESTS AT COURT

NEKAYAH HAD NOT forgotten the wise and good Elphenor, with whom she so often conversed during her residence at the fortress: she entreated her brother to send for him to court: "His piety," said she, "will assist our devotion, and his charity direct our benevolence. I have observed, with concern, that your palace is filled with men who, under the venerable garb of priesthood, are not only subject to every passion of the courtier, but are even the great springs that set in motion all the petty intrigues and invidious cabals that infest the dwelling of princes: some who, without a blush, live in open contempt of those maxims which they are obliged to inculcate, whose ostentation vies with the dignity of the prince, and whose gaiety, not to say libertinism, equals that of your emirs, and of the officers of your guards. These are indeed greatly hurtful to religion; for, though their precepts are good, there is a want of example to enforce them; yet these have often charity and often talents, and appear less dangerous than their brethren of another class, who edify the people with the exterior of rigid virtue and warm devotion, who, alike with their airy rivals, wish for despotic influence, and who pursue it by closer, and therefore more destructive methods: these are the men most to be feared; and all are surely unworthy of the station they enjoy. We have need of some pious man who may regulate the duties of devotion, and reform the many abuses introduced: such a one, as I have often told you, is to be found in Elphenor: his humility is not to be tainted by this air of infection, and his wisdom and piety are only equalled by his experience."

"Nekayah!" answered Rasselas, "I know the rectitude of thy heart, and the purity of thy intentions: I confess that great abuses have been introduced into the practices of worship, and greater still among the ministers; but Heaven protect me from ever erecting myself into a judge of religious causes! To rouse the sleeping demon of fanaticism in my dominions, would be the greatest error I could commit in administration: this must inevitably be the case, were I to attempt a reform by authoritative measures: every command would be considered as an innovation, every regulation would become a source of controversy. In all civil, all moral considerations, controversy is useful; it maintains independency of spirit, and diffuses light over a nation; but in matters of religion, it is the most dangerous of fiends. All I mean to do, and all I can do with prudence, is to give, as far as human frailty will admit, the example of unaffected constancy in the duties of piety; to discountenance equally dissipation and superstition in the ministers of the altar; to choose for the higher offices, those of the most unblemished principles, and to exclude all from any influence in civil or political affairs. As for Elphenor, of whom I believe what you have told me, I will, in consequence of that belief, promote him to one of the first dignities of his profession, where his example and his precepts may enlighten and improve the district committed to his care; but I am persuaded, when my sister reflects, she will agree with me, that more cannot, and ought not to be expected from a man of his function."

In consequence of this determination, a message was dispatched to the fortress, inviting Elphenor to court, and assuring him of the intentions of the emperor in his favour, from a conviction of the good which he would diffuse in a situation of more extensive influence. This mandate was accompanied by a letter from Nekayah, in which she returned him thanks for the consolation he had afforded her by his visits at the fortress, and expressed her desire of seeing him a witness of her happiness, as he had been of her affliction.

Chapter 41

HISTORY OF ELPHENOR

THE MESSENGER soon returned to Nekayah with the following letter.

"Think not, most esteemed lady! that I am insensible of the honour which your royal brother would confer on me, or of the kindness with which you repay what was merely a duty, consoling virtue in affliction.

"Neither suppose me neglectful of my sacred ministry, if I decline to act in a more extensive sphere, where Heaven might bless my endeavours with diffusing good over an ampler space than the narrow limits of this fortress.

"Believe me, princess! neither indolence nor ingratitude prevents me from accepting this splendid offer. Vouchsafe to peruse my history: it is neither long nor eventful: I did not choose to relate it during your residence here; your mind then required rather to be calmed than agitated by adventitious impressions.

"I am descended from no ignoble family; and followed the example of my forefathers, by serving the emperor in the field: I was crowned with conquest in a successful engagement, and should probably have continued the pursuit of military honours, had it not been for a calamity, the remembrance of which time has never been able to efface. I loved and was beloved; – but, at the moment in which I was to have been united to the object of my affection, an awful event separated us – a flash of lightning reduced my bride to ashes as she received my vows at the altar. – I will not expatiate on so dreadful a circumstance, but leave the heart of Nekayah to judge of my feelings. After a long conflict between despair and resignation, I sought consolation in visiting and comforting the afflicted: I embraced the sacred ministry, and have consecrated my life to Heaven, which forbade me to seek a refuge in the grave.

"I have been repaid for my sufferings by the blessing conferred on my endeavours: the flock, of which I am become the shepherd, love me, and find in my advice a resource against mortifications and adversity. Let those, who have, from choice alone, dedicated themselves to the immediate service of the Divinity, be promoted to the supreme dignities of our order: in me it would be the height of ingratitude to abandon that duty, which has been so long the only alleviation of my sorrows.

"I have not always, it is true, remained in the state of tranquillity in which you found me: my mind naturally active, and my ambition once boundless, led me at first to seek fame, and to deafen by tumult the voice of affliction. I endeavoured by my eloquence to distinguish myself at Gonthar, and might then have obtained the honours which you now offer me; but, after viewing the splendid scene, I found it more dazzling than real: I discovered that it would not make me amends for the serenity I must relinquish. I felt that my natural sensibility might, in a narrower sphere, be turned to the consolation of those individuals, who should stand in need of my assistance, but that a heart, blasted by misfortune, was not capable of great pursuits, and that tenderness could never happily be exchanged for ambition. I retired to this fortress, where I have passed near half a century. Can I abandon my children, when my age and my declining health require that I should lose no time in giving them proofs of my affection? If my prayers can avail, I offer them up sincerely for the prosperity of my sovereign, for that of Nekayah, and of Dinarbas. − This young hero has ever been the object of my regard: I watched his growing virtues: I once thought they were recompensed by a glorious death, before he had known misfortune. I now see they are rewarded in a different manner: it has pleased Heaven, that he should contribute to the preservation of his country, and that he should be crowned with glory and with love: few, very few, can hope for so singular a blessing! May you both long enjoy it! and ever recall to your memory, that Heaven seems to have particularly distinguished you, because your passions were made subservient to the voice of reason and virtue! May you, as the greatest felicity I can wish you, be taken both at the same instant, to the blissful habitations of permanent security! For, in the midst of transport, Nekayah must remember that all happiness in this world is transitory, except virtue, and that while she retains her steady attachment to that heavenly guide, she can want no earthly director to point out to her the celestial enjoyments of piety and beneficence."

Chapter 42

THE UTILITY OF LEARNING

THE CARES OF GOVERNMENT had too much engrossed Rasselas to permit him to enjoy, as formerly, the conversation of Imlac and the astronomer: one evening, as these were assembled with Nekayah, Zilia, and Pekuah, in a small palace of the emperor, the gardens of which overlooked the river, Rasselas joined them, with Amalphis.

"You are not to think, my friends," said the monarch, "that your society is less dear to me than formerly, or that my heart is less sensible of the charms of literary and social converse. I have found an empire in such confusion, that every branch of its government demands immediate attention; but I hope it will not be long before I may again enjoy the delights I have ever found in your company. I shall likewise require your assistance for the benefit of my subjects; you have talents to be useful; and a long intercourse with you has convinced me that your hearts are warm in every virtuous pursuit. You are not unacquainted with my notions on the necessity of learning in a state: the Abissinians in general want neither acuteness nor application, but their studies have been hitherto wrong directed: as a proof of this, we have only to consider the famous libraries, which are the source of vanity to our nation, and of envy to our neighbours. Of what are they chiefly composed? Of manuscripts, which have no other merit than the claim of dubious antiquity; treatises on mystical devotion, or judicial astrology, and annals of nations, from whom we can gain little instruction, because they were not further advanced than ourselves. I know, Imlac, you already hear me with impatience, and would except, in my general censure, the beautiful and affecting pastorals composed by the wandering Arab, from the view of simple nature, and the ideas analogous to his state of life; but these, you will yourself confess, do not much improve the learning of a people."

"If they do not immediately improve the learning," answered Imlac, "they form the taste, which I hold to be a considerable step towards it."

"I too," said the astronomer, "must speak in favour of a part of your libraries, consisting of numberless volumes which prove that the revolutions of the planets, and the division of the stars into constellations, were known to the ancients, and that modern astronomy is rather a revival than a discovery, perhaps even an imperfect revival. Probably these remaining treasures of antiquity may not be sufficient to explain to us wholly the system of the heavens; had they been so, the sages, who examined them, would have been capable of putting an end to the doubts which still arise amidst our most penetrating enquiries. But they convince us of the application and researches of former ages; they lead us to wish for a knowledge of the productions of times still more remote, and to accompany that wish with endeavours to investigate the origin of a science, founded, it is true, on nature and observation, but not susceptible of perfection without great labour and astonishing perspicacity. I do not mean from this to infer that astronomy, though one of the noblest of studies, deserves the immediate attention of a monarch, who has to form an infant nation: there are other parts of the mathematics far more essential, for which public masters should be established: such are the mechanics, hydraulics, and in short every thing that contributes to introduce simplicity into the construction of machines, to spare labour, and to improve agriculture: all which advantages can no otherwise be attained, than by a knowledge of the mathematics."

"I shall be always ready," answered Rasselas, "to promote in my dominions the study of the sciences; and, though thy modesty has been sparing of praise to thy favourite contemplations, I shall not be neglectful of them. For thee, Imlac, thou hast long known my veneration for learning: no instruction equals that obtained by the perusal of history; but how far dost thou think this study should be carried by the generality of mankind? Are not most men devoted[45] to pass their lives in one spot; and is not the history of their own country, if they mean to be useful to it, the only one necessary for them?"

---

[45]*devoted*: doomed.

Chapter 43

THE SAME SUBJECT CONTINUED

"I AM FAR FROM being of that opinion," said Imlac, "he who would confine his knowledge to one particular kingdom, would fancy it, as experience often shews us, superior to every other, and consequently think nothing could be added to its advantages: his ideas thus restrained would be incapable of forming extensive designs or plans of general utility. We cannot learn how to act in the various circumstances of life, without considering various examples, and how can we find all these in the limited boundaries of one country? We must have very little judgment if we cannot discriminate those parts of history which are applicable to our situation; and, though we would not be Romans at Constantinople, or Abissinians at Venice, we may, even from conditions directly opposite to our own, gain instruction and improvement, as we receive by reflection the light of the sun, when its rays are directed to the moon. General history is therefore, in my opinion, useful to all, and for this purpose it is necessary to have a competent knowledge of different languages, without which we are obliged to see through the false medium of translation;[46] or, what is still worse, to rely implicitly on the faith of our own historians. The Abissinians have few works of this nature, and even if they had many, it is most probable they would be infected with the same partiality and prejudices, which we find in the volumes of other nations. The only method of discovering truth is to compare these different narrations; to study the character of the people described, and of the author who describes them; to enter into their views, and adopt their feelings, but not suffer ourselves to be led astray either by the charms of eloquence, or by any apparent connexion with our own systems and interests.

"Poetry, as it teaches the knowledge of the heart, and develops the powers of the imagination, is not only pleasing, but instructive in the

---

[46]Knight learned to read and write ten languages (Elliott-Drake, 139).

great study of morality, the most essential of all, that to which all learning tends, and without which learning is of no avail."[47]

"I am perfectly persuaded," replied Rasselas, "that such is the use, and such the necessity of learning to polish the manners, and rectify the principles of a nation, that I shall ever consider it as my duty to encourage all men of letters, and to distinguish more particularly with my protection those, who by their talents and assiduity have acquired the glorious pre-eminence of enlightening, and improving their fellow-citizens."

Amalphis smiled at the expression of Rasselas, which Imlac observing, said, "I see Amalphis is not of opinion that men of letters are always the promoters of learning, if I am not mistaken in the interpretation of that smile."

"You are right, Imlac," said Amalphis, "I honour and esteem men of letters, while they retain that character; but when they make their talents subservient either to base adulation, or to the rage of party, they lose all their merit in my eyes; besides, their petty jealousies are more disgraceful than those of women, because we always expect that some philosophy and elevation of thought should be found in those minds that have been cultivated by study and instruction: I may safely say this to you, Imlac, whose pen has neither flattered nor insulted, and who have only known envy by being the object of it."

"I hope in some measure," said Rasselas, "to guard my literary subjects against the practice of adulation, by shewing them it would be lost on me; and I may perhaps diminish the fuel of envy, by giving equal encouragement to those who equally deserve. If envy could be destroyed, satire and malevolence would be unknown; for no man takes pains to dispraise him, from whom he fears no competition: but, if an angel reigned in Abissinia, he could not remedy this evil, and all my endeavours will only serve to palliate what can never be eradicated.

"There is another circumstance which Amalphis might have remarked, and which only his partiality to me has omitted. Most sovereigns, who have been particularly attached to letters, have given themselves wholly up to the delightful seduction, and have neglected their council-chamber and their camp, for their closet and their

---

[47]Compare *Rasselas*, chapter 10; see also chapter 44.

library. He who sacrifices his time, even to innocent pursuits, when they call him off from his duty, is criminal; but he is praiseworthy when he makes these pursuits tend to the great object which he must ever keep in view. I must therefore sedulously arm myself against the charms of music, painting, sculpture, and architecture, the embellishments of life, the delight of rational minds, and active imaginations. A monarch should in this imitate the sun, whose rays bestow colour and radiancy on the flowers which spring up beneath his influence, but who stops not his fiery chariot to contemplate their beauty, lest he should endanger the safety of the universe, to which it is his essential office to communicate light and heat. Such should be the conduct of the prince; in this, as in many things, less happy than his subjects, who may innocently employ their hours to attain perfection in whatever study they have made their peculiar choice, while he should have a general knowledge of all, without sacrificing his life to any in particular, however useful or pleasing."

Chapter 44

EDUCATION

"I HAVE BEEN LISTENING attentively to all your conversation," said Pekuah, "and nothing but my respect for the emperor would have kept me from interrupting Amalphis, when he spoke in so contemptuous a manner of the jealousies of women. Our sovereign thinks the conduct of the patron may increase, or diminish the envy that subsists between men of letters, and I am persuaded that the jealousy of women is fomented by the influence of men."

"I believe," answered Amalphis, "that none are more sensible of the merit of women than the military man, who can best defend them, and who, if he has any good principles, will be tender of their honour, because he feels the nicety of his own. It is true, I spoke with some contempt of the jealousy of women: whatever is the cause, we know it equally reigns over the recluse, whom we should suppose devoted to meditation, and the thoughtless, whom we might imagine busied only in gaiety. Cast your eyes on a company of children; they have not to accuse men of raising the passion of envy by flattery, yet never does it operate more forcibly than in their infant breasts: all causes are capable of bringing to light this fatal evil with those in whom it is unfortunately inherent, and none but great minds are totally exempt from it.

"The good or the bad dispositions of women have a very extensive influence in society, and could we be so fortunate as to discover the motives of what we call by the general name of caprice, we might probably succeed in preventing the effects. Empires have been ruined by the jealousies of women; to them are owing many of the great revolutions that have decided the fate of nations; and if we join to theirs the sacerdotal influence, I fancy we shall prove that statesmen and conquerors have often been simply the machines put in motion by weak hands, and versatile heads."

"If women," said Imlac, "frequently do great hurt by interposing in affairs which seem foreign to their sex, how useful are they when they turn their thoughts to the education of their children, and by these domestic and natural cares provide happiness in future, not only for themselves but for their country! The first impressions are difficult to efface, and the first impressions are given by women; their mistaken tenderness has formed cowards, and their capricious anger has reared up tyrants. If therefore they deserve our censure for the ill qualities which their children have imbibed from them, let us not deny them our praises for many of the virtues which make men an honour to their age and to their nation."

"When I think on education," said Rasselas, "I wander in a labyrinth, from which I know not how to extricate myself, and yet every delay to pursue this important subject seems to accuse me of criminal omission. From faulty or neglected education spring the evils which I am labouring to correct at present, and which I would endeavour to obviate for the future.

"Private education, I believe, in general, to be pernicious to men, because it is the way to perpetuate the failings of the race from one generation to another; for how can he teach wisely, who has not been wisely taught? It seems more expedient that the public should form those by whose service it is to be benefited – but what is the public? It is a name without a determined idea, in which, though all individuals are interested, few think themselves immediately concerned. If so small a number of parents are found capable of educating their own children, are we to expect that more attention will be paid to this duty by persons who have no tie for the performance of it, but that of general utility, or self interest?"

"The great advantages of public education," said Imlac, "are these: proper rules are formed, and blind tenderness is not likely to interfere with their execution: the children have the benefit of reciprocal emulation, and of some initiation into a knowledge of the world: this, I own, is too frequently attended by an early acquaintance with vice; but could not this be remedied by a prudent choice of masters? The greatest model of this sort is the Lacedæmonian school, which was imperfect only in what was ill-planned from the first:[48] the institution was rigorously followed, and therefore if wise rules are made, they can be strictly observed."

---

[48]State-controlled, compulsory education for all boys and girls in ancient Sparta (Lacedæmon) emphasized physical training.

"I depend greatly on thee, Imlac," returned the prince, "for the formation of such rules; thou hast not only read, but seen much, and the great fault I have remarked in those who preside over the education of youth, is their total ignorance of those scenes for which they are to prepare their disciples."

Chapter 45

FALSE PRETENSIONS TO KNOWLEDGE

"As for myself," said Pekuah, "I would willingly undertake to teach children what little I have myself attained: I know no happiness in knowledge without communication, but I must be permitted to choose my scholars: to instruct those who have genius is delightful, but to drive ideas into minds incapable of making them spread or fructify, is a torment which none but wretched preceptors know."

"Lady," said the astronomer, "all are not so happy in pupils as the Arab[49] and myself; yet I know too well the sweetness of your temper not to believe you would think your pains well rewarded, if they succeeded in fixing the giddy to application, or in enlivening the apathy of dulness."

"Such a task," interrupted Nekayah, "is worthy of your beneficence and talents, but I own myself of the opinion of Pekuah – who can make feathers solid, or lead elastic?"

"Madam," replied the astronomer, "though their qualities cannot be changed, they may be directed to useful purposes."

"True," said Amalphis, "the feather may, by being applied to the arrow guide its intended flight; and the lead, formed into a shot, will reach the destined mark from the musket; this may be called their education, without which the feather would have fluttered useless in the air, and the lead remained unheeded on the ground. The misfortune is, that weak and sordid minds are sometimes employed in great attempts; to this fatal error we owe thoughtless or indolent statesmen, and tedious or delusive writers. It were much to be wished that servile offices could be left to mean capacities, and that none should act the first parts on the great theatre of the world, but those who have talents to fill the character. All men may be made useful, if they are placed in their proper station, and their faculties directed to those pursuits of which they are most capable."

---

[49]Pekuah studied astronomy with her Arab captor (*Rasselas*, chapter 39).

"As for utility," resumed Imlac, "few parents reflect whether the education which they give their sons, will make them serviceable to their country, or to their fellow creatures: they wish that it may enable them to shine in society, and they early inspire them with a desire of shewing all the learning of which they are possessed. As vanity has been the motive of his education, the same disposition attends the unfortunate youth through life: perhaps he finds himself unequal to support, without further study, the reputation of that instruction which he pretends to have received: he therefore seeks the resource of nomenclature,[50] syllabus, and compilation, which keep him for ever immersed in ignorance and impertinence.

"Such are the steps of those who affect knowledge, members of society far more insupportable than the rustic or the trifler; men who have no original ideas, no solid erudition, and yet mix boldly with the learned, while they impose on the untaught. Even serious application, diligent study, and sound judgment must wait long in the vestibule of learning, before they can be admitted to her sanctuary."

---

[50]*nomenclature*: "A vocabulary; a dictionary."

Chapter 46

THE CONVERSATION TURNS ON VARIOUS MATTERS

IMLAC HERE INTERRUPTED his discourse, on perceiving that Rasselas was not listening to him, but that his thoughts were employed on some idea which he seemed unwilling to communicate.

"I was thinking," said the prince, "how miserable we should be, if Heaven was to grant us what we have fondly desired at a former period of our lives.[51] Do you remember, while we were detained in Egypt by the inundations of the Nile, that Pekuah, delighted with the convent of St. Anthony, wished to be prioress of an order of pious maidens, and there fix her invariable residence? yet Pekuah is contented with the diversity of life that has since been her lot, and would not, I fancy, be willing to relinquish the court of the princess, where her mind enjoys rational amusement in the society of Amalphis, Imlac, and her astronomical instructor; and where the liveliness of her wit finds constant exercise in the different groups that compose the motly scene in the mansion of a sovereign."

"Certainly," answered Pekuah, "I have at present no wish for retirement: while I was lately imprisoned with the princess in the valley, I often wondered how I should have ever desired to become the inhabitant of a monastery, and reflected where I could have found nuns whose society would have been comparable to that of Nekayah; and yet, even with that society so dear to me, I longed to be again at liberty."

"And you, sister," said Rasselas, "would you be greatly delighted, if Heaven should make you directress of a college of learned ladies; and would you renounce the society of Dinarbas, and your friends, for the pleasure of discoursing with the aged, and instructing the young? As for myself, I wished for a little kingdom, and was ever extending the limits of my fancied dominions: I now find the government of Abissinia an arduous task, and though nothing should

---

[51]See *Rasselas*, chapter 49; *fondly*: "Foolishly, injudiciously."

induce me to renounce what it is my duty to retain, I see in the friendship of Zilia, and the esteem of those around me, the summit of my happiness, a happiness totally independent on the charms of royalty. Such were our wishes, Nekayah! thou and Pekuah should return thanks to Heaven that yours were not accomplished, and I, that blessings were bestowed on me, which alone could make the accomplishment of mine supportable."

"I feel the force of your observation, my brother," answered the princess, "but circumstances are perpetually changing, and we are not responsible for the influence which they may have on our minds. Imlac and the astronomer, it is true, were wiser; they made no choice, because they had experienced how little we know in this world what is best for us. I believe, however, we may venture to affirm, that they who condemn themselves to irrevocable retirement, are greatly deceived in their expectations, and if their repentance is not manifest, it is because pride will not allow them to own it.

"I think I should have been sufficiently mistress of myself to bear with resignation the misfortunes of which I had once the gloomy prospect; but I am certain I could never have hoped for so great felicity as Providence has been pleased unexpectedly to grant me."

"It is singular," said the astronomer, "that those whose imagination is most lively, are generally the most subject to occasional disgust and dejection, and consequently most led to seek a refuge in solitude; whether their spirits are more worn by greater exertion, or whether a mind naturally active, takes a stronger impulse whatever way it tends."

"I believe," said Pekuah, "such minds want constant employment, and feel more pain from inaction than from misfortune: indeed, listless indifference is the most insupportable of all situations. I know, that when I am deprived of the society of those who can entertain and instruct me, I prefer the intercourse of beings whose follies or singularities are of the ridiculous kind, to those in whom I can find nothing to blame or commend, who weary me with insipidity, and yet afford no theme for amusing my friends at their expence."

"The arms of ridicule are very dangerous, Pekuah," said the princess, "I confess thou hast often used them with dexterity, and I cannot deny that I have taken pleasure in thy sallies; but consider what pain they may give to the innocent, what enemies they may create among the vindictive!"

"And yet, if we were deprived of ridicule," said Imlac, "we should lose much of the power of wit, and much of the influence of general opinion – two invisible monarchs, who govern with sufficient justice, and who, if they do not prevent crimes, at least may reform errors."

Chapter 47

SIMPLICITY

"IMLAC," SAID RASSELAS, "I have often observed with what skill those who possess the advantages of a superior education and knowledge of the world, can, without apparent incivility, lessen, in his own opinion, that man who has intruded himself on their company, or who has abused the privileges they have allowed him: he has no reason to complain, yet he feels himself uneasy in their presence, and is awed into respect without the shame of reproof.

"This is one of the many advantages of good-breeding – a quality which has perhaps more power than any other, since it will for a time conceal even want of talents, and want of virtue. How necessary is it therefore to acquire this pleasing pre-eminence, without which the most essential endowments are abashed before inferior merit. Politeness may be called the portrait of virtue, and its resemblance is so perfect, that nothing but the solidity of the original is wanting: ceremony and affectation are poor imitators of true good-breeding, which is easy and simple, like nature itself. If I was to form a system, it would be that of simplicity; it should pervade all works of imagination, all enquiries of science, all performances of the chisel and pencil, all behaviour, and all dress. Carry this idea even to the most awful height, what is simplicity, but truth, the great basis of virtue and religion? When I call this a system, it is only to comply with the common mode of speech, which would make of the most natural ideas a philosophical discovery. Simplicity is the child of nature: the love of it seems implanted in us by Providence; yet all the labour of erring mortals is to depart from this great and open road, and to return to it when they have seen the fallacy of winding paths, and doubtful mazes."

"My brother," said Nekayah, "when you extol with reason the universal merit of simplicity, you certainly do not mean to imply a neglect of combination of ideas in the works of art or science, or a neglect of common forms in dress or manners."

"So far from it," replied the prince, "that as nature is varied, so must be the imitation or investigation of it; and to affect singularity, either in habit or behaviour, would be wandering from the very rule that I have been proposing."

"To explain this," said Imlac, "we need only have recourse to our own feelings and perceptions: the variety of nature is infinite; but it is harmonized by general effect. The verdant leaves of the trees participate of the azure of the sky, and their trunks of the colouring of the earth: the most discordant sounds in music, the most distant ideas in metaphysics, are combined by gradation, or opposed by contrast; yet even in contrast there is an imperceptible connexion that unites the whole. Without one great plan, to which all is subservient, our general conduct in life, and our finest productions of art or genius, are like a republic without laws, or a monarchy without a king.

"Simplicity, by those whose wayward minds are not susceptible of its charms, is supposed to exclude pomp and elegance; yet what is pomp without dignity, and elegance without grace? Both are the offspring of nature, and sisters to simplicity."

"I know," said Zilia, "that no other power obtains access to our hearts: the various inflexions of voice, the painful[52] efforts of the musician, who shows his art in deviating from nature, excite our wonder; but the nightingale, and he whose notes are equally pathetic and simple, inspire us with more than admiration."

"If our sovereign introduces simplicity at court," said Pekuah, "what will become of the numberless artists, merchants, and other abettors of luxury, that owe their chief support to the inhabitants of this mansion, and to the influence of their example over the rest of the nation?"

"The circulation of riches, for the gratification of pride, indolence, or the love of pleasure," replied the prince, "is, in my opinion, detrimental to a kingdom. I have often thought, that every ingot, stored by commerce in the treasury of a monarch, has cost him the virtue and principles of a subject. The romantic warmth of youth, may perhaps make me judge too severely; and it is possible that commerce may, in some nations, be carried on without insidious treaties between the respective governments, and without unjust attempts of individuals to make their fortunes at the expence of their

---

[52]*painful*: "Difficult; requiring labour."

neighbours. Though I love virtue too well not to wish that I could be persuaded of its general influence in every station of life, yet I shall never consider luxury at best but as a necessary evil, and its dependant, commerce, as a very dangerous trial for the principles of its followers. – Nothwithstanding this conviction, I cannot abolish either: money is wanted in all states, that they may not become the prey of their richer neighbours; commerce must therefore be encouraged; but it is our duty to endeavour, as far as we are able, to prevent fraud and monopoly. Were it possible for any monarch to render a people perfectly happy in themselves, it would not be sufficient; he must make the whole world participate in the great reformation, or he could never preserve his own subjects in security. We may indulge ideal speculation, but experience shows us this humiliating truth, that all we can do is to diminish evil and to promote good, by the means that are given us: perfect justice can alone by exercised by the Divinity."

Chapter 48

DINARBAS RETURNS FROM THE COURT OF THE SULTAN

THE CONVERSATION was here interrupted by the arrival of Dinarbas from Constantinople. He was received with great joy by the sovereign, by his father, Nekayah, and Zilia: but Amalphis was impatient to know the success of his embassy; he considered that the honour of his son was engaged, and anxiously entreated him to begin his narration.

"When I arrived at Constantinople," said Dinarbas, "I found the sultan highly incensed at the independent answer of the Abissinian monarch, and displeased with me for not having warmly seconded his proposal of a treaty: he declared that nothing should persuade him to relinquish pretensions which he thought justly founded on the assistance he had furnished: he said, that Rasselas owed to him alone the throne of Abissinia, and could not, without ingratitude, refuse to comply with his demands.

"In answer to this, I observed, that when I had first recourse to him for assistance, the prince was totally ignorant of my intentions; that afterwards, the army marched without my knowledge, and expressly contrary to the wishes of Rasselas; that a happy change had indeed been effected by their intervention, but that the whole nation joined in restoring their former sovereign; and that, had Rasselas, instead of Menas, headed the troops of Abissinia, the victory might not have been so easily obtained.

"The sultan would not listen to my remonstrances: he denounced war against my country, but accompanied his denunciation with a desire that I would remain in his council, and retain the government of Servia, both which I refused, and prepared to depart from Constantinople, offended with myself for having indulged the romantic idea, that a man at the head of a powerful and submissive nation, would listen to the voice of justice, against what he supposed his own interest: I said to myself, that I had mistaken in him magnificence for generosity, and splendid professions for honourable sentiments.

"Being on the point of leaving his dominions, I again requested an audience, that I might testify my gratitude for the favours which he had conferred on me, and my regret for not being able to retain them without infidelity to my natural sovereign: he seemed affected, and, commanding his attendants to withdraw, spoke to me in the following manner.

"'Dinarbas! I love thee, and will say to thee, what I would not say to any other man. I believe thee – read these letters, and tell me whether they are genuine.'

"So saying, he gave into my hands the letters which your majesty, the princess, and myself had sent by the messenger to my father and Zilia, the loss of which we always suspected to have been owing to the Turks. 'These letters,' continued the sultan, 'have just been delivered to me – I wait thy answer.'

"I easily convinced him that they were really sent from the court of Abissinia; on which he made me this reply.

"'Dinarbas! I perceive that truth, honour, and integrity ought not only in individuals, but in governments, to be the great ruling principles of action: I learn by these letters the real sentiments of thy sovereign, his innocence in his steps to the throne, and the firmness of his character: were I to make war against him, the event would at least be doubtful on my side, and the disgrace inevitable. His army is better disciplined than mine, and I know not whether any superiority of number would weigh against the attachment of his troops to a warlike sovereign, and a tender father: I cannot boast of either of these titles, nor have I energy sufficient to deserve them; but the fatal delusion of flattery, which seems to have enchanted this imperial seat, has not so totally blinded me, as to prevent me from revering in others the virtues of which I am incapable: besides, my own interest engages me to retain one honest man in my dominions, and to cultivate a friendship with one disinterested prince. Return to Abissinia, offer my alliance to thy monarch on equal terms, lead back my army, and teach me how to govern.'

"I was astonished and affected at the sultan's discourse. Does not this man deserve to be virtuous?"

Chapter 49

MARRIAGES OF RASSELAS AND NEKAYAH

"THE INTERCEPTION of our letters," said Rasselas, "has then informed the sultan of the purity of my intentions, and of the loyalty of my subjects; how frequently have I wished that my inmost thoughts could be known! Guilt and innocence so often wear the same aspect, that far from fearing the secret emissaries who may be placed to observe my conduct, I only desire that they should report the truth.

"To thee, Dinarbas, we owe the tranquillity of the empire; and in thy friendship I have found more than a recompense for all my searches after happiness; but how can I estimate the felicity that is promised me in the society of my Zilia! A felicity which was once beyond my hopes, but without which, I now could not exist. I remember that I had formerly with Nekayah a long debate on marriage, in which we could not decide whether early or late unions, whether sympathy or reason were most conducive to conjugal happiness:[53] we have, by a singular course of events, been permitted to enjoy at once these opposite advantages: the warmest affection has been confirmed by the severest trials: surely we have before us the fairest prospect, a prospect to which neither interested views, nor transitory passion can lay claim."

"In this," said the astronomer, "your virtues are rewarded; he who wants firmness deserves not success; reason can be no enemy to that love, which is founded on virtue, and supported by constancy."

The nuptials of Rasselas and Zilia, Dinarbas and Nekayah, were celebrated without ostentatious magnificence, but with a dignity becoming their rank. The poor had the greatest share in the rejoicings, because the superfluous treasures, consumed on similar occasions, were distributed among them. It was decided that Dinarbas should in a few weeks conduct back the army of the sultan into his dominions; that he should, with Nekayah, fix his residence in

---

[53]See *Rasselas*, chapters 28-29.

Servia, but that their visits to Abissinia should be frequent. Pekuah was to accompany the princess, and the astronomer, delighted in varying the scene, since he had tasted the charms of society, begged leave to visit the states of Dinarbas, who, with Nekayah, gladly acceded to his proposal: his knowledge and his virtues made them revere him as a father.

Rasselas concluded an alliance, offensive and defensive, with the sultan; repaid the expences of the troops, and graced the officers with distinguished marks of his favour.

Amalphis, honoured and beloved by his son and sovereign, applied all his care to form the Abissinian army. Imlac was no less attentive to the institutions of Rasselas, for promoting learning in his dominions: both enjoyed the confidence of the monarch: but neither did Amalphis receive the memorials of the officers of the army, nor Imlac the dedications of the poets: every matter was first referred to the emperor, who consulted those, whom he had appointed to be the heads of the several departments of the state, before he gave his answer, but did not always decide according to their judgment.

Zilia never interfered in public business; her voice often directed establishments of charity, and her taste frequently decided on the protection to be given to genius.

Innocent gaiety, and rational amusements, were introduced by her into the court of Abissinia; her dress was simple and elegant, and consisted of the manufactures of the country: she distinguished no woman as her favourite, but shewed peculiar regard to all those whose conduct was exemplary, without affectation, and whose minds were well informed without vain pretensions to a display of learning. Her beneficence was extended to all, and if she shewed any partiality, it was to the orphans and widows of those who had served their country in battle; for she did not forget that she was the daughter of Amalphis: she knew the heartfelt misery of that disappointed hope and poverty, which honest pride forbids to own; the lot of many families, whose chiefs have bravely supported the honour of their prince and country.[54]

---

[54]Knight's mother, the widow of a Rear-Admiral, hoped and schemed fruitlessly for a government pension, which she believed her "just due," to supplement her small income (Elliott-Drake, 195; Luttrell, 37-38).

Chapter 50

VISIT TO THE HAPPY VALLEY

BEFORE THE DEPARTURE of Dinarbas and Nekayah, Rasselas and his friends made a visit to the happy valley. The prince and his sister wished to review those scenes, which had been to them the objects of satiety at one time, and of uneasiness at another; they returned to every spot which remembrance had dignified, and rejoiced to contemplate those situations which were once irksome to their imagination.

Rasselas had only one brother left, a youth whose education he recommended to the care of Imlac: he freed the princesses, his sisters, from the confinement of the valley, and gave them permission either to remain there, or return with him to Gonthar. He commanded the massy gates that closed the entrance of the valley to be destroyed; the dancers, musicians, and other professors of arts, merely of amusement, to be dismissed with pensions, and liberty to be granted to all.

The prince, followed by his companions, led Zilia to the entrance of the cavern, through which he had first made his escape. "Consider this cavity," said he, "and think what must be the grateful transports that glow in my breast – ; Nekayah! Imlac! Pekuah! is not our search rewarded? Let us return thanks to Heaven for having inspired us with that active desire of knowledge, and contempt of indolence, that have blessed us with instruction, with friendship, and with love! It is true that we have been singularly favoured by Providence; and few can expect, like us, to have their fondest wishes crowned with success; but even when our prospects were far different, our search after happiness had taught us resignation: let us therefore warn others against viewing the world as a scene of inevitable misery. Much is to be suffered in our journey through life; but conscious virtue, active fortitude, the balm of sympathy, and submission to the Divine Will, can support us through the painful trial. With them every station is the best; without them prosperity is a feverish dream, and pleasure a poisoned cup.

"Youth will vanish, health will decay, beauty fade, and strength sink into imbecility; but if we have enjoyed their advantages, let us not say there is no good, because the good in this world is not permanent: none but the guilty are excluded from at least temporary happiness; and if he whose imagination is lively, and whose heart glows with sensibility, is more subject than others to poignant grief and maddening disappointment, surely he will confess that he has moments of ecstacy and consolatory reflection that repay him for all his sufferings.

"Let us now return to the busy scene of action where we are called, and endeavour, by the exercise of our several duties, to deserve a continuation of the blessings which Providence has granted, and on the use of which depends all our present, all our future felicity."

FINIS